ELIOT'S BOOK *of* BOOKISH LISTS

Henry Eliot

* *

✣ ✣

§ §

◇ ◇

☚ ☚ ☚ ☚ ☚ ☚ ☚ ☚ ☚ ☚ ☚ ☚ ☚ ☚ ☚

••• ••• ••• ••• ••• ••• ••• ••• ••• ••• ••• ••• ••• ••• ••• •••

¶ ¶

» »

—·—·—·—·—·—·—·—·—·—·—·—·—·—·—

v ^ v ^ v ^ v ^ v ^ v ^ v ^ v ^ v ^ v ^ v ^ v ^ v ^ v ^ v

••• ••• ••• ••• ••• ••• ••• ••• ••• ••• ••• ••• ••• ••• ••• •••

☛ ☛ ☛ ☛ ☛ ☛ ☛ ☛ ☛ ☛ ☛ ☛ ☛ ☛ ☛

□ □

➳ ➳ ➳ ➳ ➳ ➳ ➳ ➳ ➳ ➳ ➳ ➳ ➳ ➳ ➳ ➳ ➳ ➳

“ “

ELIOT'S
BOOK
of
BOOKISH
LISTS

HENRY ELIOT

PARTICULAR BOOKS*

* An imprint of Penguin Books

list, *n.*	pleasure, joy, delight[†]	
list, *n.*	a strip of cloth	
list, *n.*	the ear[†]	
list, *n.*	the mark of a wound[†]	
list, *n.*	a stripe of colour[†]	
lists, *n.*	a scene of combat	
list, *n.*	the inclination of a ship to one side	
list, *n.*	a catalogue consisting of a series of names, figures, words, or the like	
list, *n.*	a long piece of gammon[†]	
list, *n.*	the titles of books published by a particular publisher	

[†] These definitions are now obsolete, although their sense survives in words such as 'listless', 'listel' and 'listen'.

Five thousand years ago, humans invented writing in order to write lists: the earliest writing systems in Mesopotamia were devised to record lists of livestock on clay tablets. ¶ 'The list is the origin of culture,' said Umberto Eco, when he curated an exhibition of lists for the Musée du Louvre. 'It's part of the history of art and literature. What does culture want? To make infinity comprehensible. [...] And how, as a human being, does one face infinity? How does one attempt to grasp the incomprehensible? Through lists.' ¶ Shopping lists, to-do lists, wish lists, bucket lists – we all make lists every day. They can be as prosaic as laundry and as poetic as birdsong. ¶ 'How do I love thee?' asked Elizabeth Barrett Browning in a sonnet. 'Let me count the ways.' Lovers frequently turn to lists to express the inexpressible. In Virginia Woolf's novel, for example, Orlando compares a seductive young boy to 'a melon, a pineapple, an olive tree, an emerald, and a fox in the snow' in the space of three seconds. ¶ The paradox and perhaps the pleasure of the list is that it's both finite and infinite. Each element is discrete but the list implies connection and there-fore a category. The more disparate the elements, the broader the implied category, until its boundaries approach the limits of our imagination. ¶ A particularly beguiling list appears in *Through the Looking-Glass* by Lewis Carroll. 'The time has come,' the Walrus says, 'To talk of many things: Of shoes – and ships – and sealing-wax – Of cabbages – and kings – And why the sea is boiling hot – And whether pigs have wings.' With seven conversational topics, the sly Walrus implies a universal discourse, but he is dazzling his audience of young oysters: in truth, he plans to eat them. ¶ 'Lists may indeed offer the reader a brief intimation of everything,' observes the novelist Francis Spufford: 'they can equally well be fierce flirtations with nothingness.' The significance of a list sometimes lies in what is omitted, in the gaps between the lines, or, as in the case of the Walrus, it may be pure misdirection. ¶ Perhaps the fundamental reason we are attracted to lists is because their promise of the infinite distracts us from the inescapable limit of our own numbered days. 'We like lists,' Eco said, 'because we don't want to die.' ¶ If that is true, then the reading list is our redemption. Books allow us to see through the eyes of others, so life ceases to be just one damned thing after another. 'Only connect ...' is E. M. Forster's epigraph to *Howards End*. ¶ 'Everything only connected by "and" and "and",' wrote Elizabeth Bishop. 'Open the book.'

It was a DARK and STORMY NIGHT...

Since 1983, the English department at San Jose State University has staged the Bulwer Lytton Fiction Contest, named after the nineteenth-century novelist Edward Bulwer Lytton, who is perhaps most famous for the first sentence of his novel *Paul Clifford*: 'It was a dark and stormy night ...'* Contestants are invited to compose the opening sentence of 'the worst of all possible novels'. Here is a selection of winning entries:

1983 WINNER

The camel died quite suddenly on the second day, and Selena fretted sulkily and, buffing her already impeccable nails – not for the first time since the journey began – pondered snidely if this would dissolve into a vignette of minor inconveniences like all the other holidays spent with Basil.

— Gail Cain, USA

1985 WINNER

The countdown had stalled at T minus 69 seconds when Desiree, the first female ape to go up in space, winked at me slyly and pouted her thick, rubbery lips unmistakably – the first of many such advances during what would prove to be the longest, and most memorable, space voyage of my career.

— Martha Simpson, USA

1992 WINNER

As the newest Lady Turnpot descended into the kitchen wrapped only in her celery-green dressing gown, her creamy bosom rising and falling like a temperamental soufflé, her tart mouth pursed in distaste, the sous-chef whispered to the scullery boy, 'I don't know what to make of her.'

— Laurel Fortuner, France

1999 WINNER

Through the gathering gloom of a late-October afternoon, along the greasy, cracked paving-stones slick from the sputum of the sky, Stanley Ruddlethorp wearily trudged up the hill from the cemetery

---

* The sentence continues: 'the rain fell in torrents, except at occasional intervals, when it was checked by a violent gust of wind which swept up the streets (for it is in London that our scene lies), rattling along the housetops, and fiercely agitating the scanty flame of the lamps that struggled against the darkness.'

where his wife, sister, brother, and three children were all buried, and forced open the door of his decaying house, blissfully unaware of the catastrophe that was soon to devastate his life.

— David Chuter, UK

2000 WINNER

The heather-encrusted Headlands, veiled in fog as thick as smoke in a crowded pub, hunched precariously over the moors, their rocky elbows slipping off land's end, their bulbous, craggy noses thrust into the thick foam of the North Sea like bearded old men falling asleep in their pints.

— Gary Dahl, USA

2008 WINNER

Theirs was a New York love, a checkered taxi ride burning rubber, and like the city, their passion was open 24/7, steam rising from their bodies like slick streets exhaling warm, moist breath through manhole covers stamped 'Forged by DeLaney Bros., Piscataway, NJ'.

— Gordon Spik, USA

2011 WINNER

Cheryl's mind turned like the vanes of a wind-powered turbine, chopping her sparrow-like thoughts into bloody pieces that fell onto a growing pile of forgotten memories.

— Sue Fondrie, USA

2014 WINNER

When the dead moose floated into view the famished crew cheered – this had to mean land! – but Captain Walgrove, flinty-eyed and clear headed thanks to the starvation cleanse in progress, gave fateful orders to remain on the original course and await the appearance of a second and confirming moose.

— Betsy Dorfman, USA

2020 WINNER

Her Dear John missive flapped unambiguously in the windy breeze, hanging like a pizza menu on the doorknob of my mind.

— Lisa Kluber, USA

2021 WINNER

A lecherous sunrise flaunted itself over a flatulent sea, ripping the obsidian bodice of night asunder with its rapacious fingers of gold, thus exposing her dusky bosom to the dawn's ogling stare.

— Stu Duval, New Zealand

The MONSTER'S LIBRARY

In Mary Shelley's *Frankenstein*, the monster learns about western civilization by studying three books, which he finds in an abandoned portmanteau.

The Sorrows of Young Werther by Johann Wolfgang von Goethe teaches the monster about domestic society and human psychology, but leaves him feeling alienated.

Plutarch's Lives elevates him above the sphere of his own reflections, teaching him about heroes, history and geography, towns and kingdoms, civic virtue, political vice, and death on the battlefield.

Paradise Lost by John Milton excites the deepest emotions. The monster compares himself to both Adam, created and alone, and Satan.

Some UNUSUAL NARRATORS

My Name Is Red by Orhan Pamuk features an array of surprising narrators, including a murdered corpse, a miniature painting of a horse, a gold coin, a tree and the colour red. Here are more novels with unusual narrators:

an angel	*What's Bred in the Bone* by Robertson Davies
a bee	*The Bees* by Laline Paull
a bowl	*The Collector Collector* by Tibor Fischer
a cat	*I Am a Cat* by Natsume Sōseki
a corpse	*The Posthumous Memoirs of Brás Cubas* by Machado de Assis
a foetus	*Nutshell* by Ian McEwan
a horse	*Black Beauty* by Anna Sewell
Qfwfq	*Cosmicomics* by Italo Calvino
a spirit-child	*The Famished Road* by Ben Okri
a stone*	*The Dream of the Red Chamber* by Cao Xueqin
a tiger	*A Tiger for Malgudi* by R. K. Narayan

* *The Dream of the Red Chamber* is narrated by a lustrous stone, the only piece of celestial masonry left over after the goddess Nüwa mended the sky. For this reason, the novel is sometimes known as *The Story of the Stone* (see p.30).

TRISTRAM'S DIGRESSIONS

'Digressions, incontestably, are the sunshine;——they are the life, the soul of reading!' In the sixth volume of Laurence Sterne's meandering novel, *The Life and Opinions of Tristram Shandy, Gentleman*, Tristram looks back at the previous volumes and illustrates the course of their rambling narrative lines (conscientiously annotating the digressions in volume five):

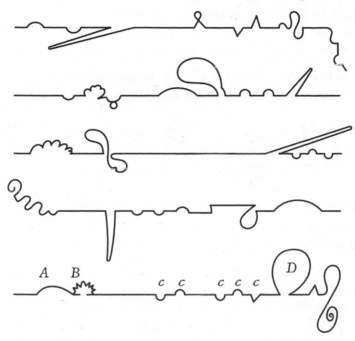

He apologizes for these parentheses, digressions, flashbacks and interpolations, but claims that – except for certain episodes – he has hardly 'stepped a yard' out of his way in the sixth volume, and promises that 'if I mend at this rate, it is not impossible [...] but I may arrive hereafter at the excellency of going on even thus:

which is a line drawn as straight as I could draw it'. Thankfully, Tristram's resolve is short-lived, and the seventh, eighth and ninth volumes turn out to be just as full of 'frisky' digressions as the rest of the novel.

BAD SEX *in* FICTION

Since 1993, the *Literary Review* has awarded an annual Bad Sex in Fiction Award to honour the year's 'most outstandingly awful scene of sexual description in an otherwise good novel'. The *Literary Review* cancelled the 2020 and 2021 awards, during the COVID-19 pandemic, because 'the public had been subjected to too many bad things [...] to justify exposing it to bad sex as well'. There have been twenty-eight winners so far:

1993	*A Time to Dance* by Melvyn Bragg ⟶	'And then we would be on the bed and I touching you, hungry. Eyes closed, fingers inside you, reaching into the melting fluid rubbered silk – a relief map of mysteries – the eager clitoris, reeking of you, our tongues imitating the fingers, your hands gripping and stroking me but also careful not to excite too much.'
1994	*The Stonebreakers* by Philip Hook	
1995	*Gridiron* by Philip Kerr	
1996	*The Big Kiss* by David Huggins	
1997	*The Matter of the Heart* by Nicholas Royle	
1998	*Charlotte Gray* by Sebastian Faulks	
1999	*Starcrossed* by A. A. Gill	
2000	*Kissing England* by Sean Thomas	
2001	*Rescue Me* by Christopher Hart	
2002	*Tread Softly* by Wendy Perriam	
2003	*Bunker 13* by Aniruddha Bahal	
2004	*I Am Charlotte Simmons* by Tom Wolfe ⟶	'Slither slither slither slither went the tongue, but the hand – that was what she tried to concentrate on, the hand, since it had the entire terrain of her torso to explore and not just the otorhinolaryngological caverns – oh God, it was not just at the border where the flesh of the breast joins the pectoral sheath of the chest – no, the hand was cupping her entire right – *Now!* She must say "No, Hoyt" and talk to him like a dog.'
2005	*Winkler* by Giles Coren	
2006	*Twenty Something* by Iain Hollingshead	
2007	*The Castle in the Forest* by Norman Mailer	
2008	*Shire Hell* by Rachel Johnson	
2009	*The Kindly Ones* by Jonathan Littell	
2010	*The Shape of Her* by Rowan Somerville	
2011	*Ed King* by David Guterson	
2012	*Infrared* by Nancy Huston	
2013	*The City of Devi* by Manil Suri	
2014	*The Age of Magic* by Ben Okri	
2015	*List of the Lost* by Morrissey	
2016	*The Day Before Happiness* by Erri De Luca	
2017	*The Destroyers* by Christopher Bollen	
2018	*Katerina* by James Frey	
2019	*The Office of Gardens and Ponds* by Didier Decoin & *Pax* by John Harvey	
2020	cancelled	
2021	cancelled	

The ODES *of* KEATS

In April and May 1819, aged twenty-three, John Keats wrote five of his six great odes; 'To Autumn' followed in September. He died seventeen months later, in a room at the foot of the Spanish Steps in Rome.

'To Psyche'	*A bright torch, and a casement ope at night*
'On a Grecian Urn'	*Beauty is truth, truth beauty*
'To a Nightingale'	*Now more than ever seems it rich to die*
'On Melancholy'	*Then glut thy sorrow on a morning rose*
'On Indolence'	*The blissful cloud of summer-indolence*
'To Autumn'	*Season of mists and mellow fruitfulness*

An ARM *and a* LEG

In *Johnny Got His Gun* by Dalton Trumbo, an American soldier wakes up in hospital to discover that he has lost his arms, legs, face and tongue in an artillery shell explosion. Here are some other literary amputees:

MISSING HANDS

Captain James Hook
right hand fed to a crocodile,
replaced by a hook, in *Peter Pan*
by J. M. Barrie

Dr Julius No
both hands removed by
a Chinese crime syndicate,
replaced by prosthetics,
in *Dr No* by Ian Fleming

Titus Andronicus
left hand cut off to pay a false
ransom, in *Titus Andronicus*
by William Shakespeare

MISSING LEGS

Captain Ahab
leg chewed off by a white whale,
wears a whalebone leg, in
Moby-Dick by Herman Melville

Long John Silver
left leg lost in a pirate sea battle,
uses a crutch, in *Treasure Island*
by Robert Louis Stevenson

Jonathan Small
right leg eaten by a crocodile
in the Ganges, wears a wooden
leg, in *The Sign of Four*
by Arthur Conan Doyle

The SCRIBLERUS CLUB

Founded in 1714, this was a group of British authors, who collaborated under the pseudonym 'Martinus Scriblerus'. The Scriblerus Club is chiefly remembered for *The Memoirs of Martinus Scriblerus*, a satire of pretentious erudition. Henry Fielding later described himself as 'Scriblerus Secundus'.

Dr John Arbuthnot · John Gay · Thomas Parnell · Alexander Pope
Henry St John, Viscount Bolingbroke · Jonathan Swift

PROUST'S INVOLUNTARY MEMORIES

Starting with the madeleine dipped in tea, the narrator of Marcel Proust's *In Search of Lost Time* has a sequence of innocuous experiences, which trigger the remembrances that form his seven-volume narrative. In *Proust*, which Samuel Beckett wrote when he was twenty-four, he lists eleven key moments that prompt the narrator's involuntary memories.

1. The madeleine steeped in an infusion of tea.
2. The steeples of Martinville, seen from Dr. Percepied's trap.
3. A musty smell in a public lavatory in the Champs-Elysées.
4. The three trees, seen near Balbec* from the carriage of Mme. de Villeparisis.
5. The hedge of hawthorn near Balbec.
6. He stoops to unbutton his boots on the occasion of his second visit to the Grand Hotel at Balbec.
7. Uneven cobbles in the courtyard of the Guermantes Hotel.
8. The noise of a spoon against a plate.
9. He wipes his mouth with a napkin.
10. The noise of water in the pipes.
11. George Sand's *François le Champi*.†

* The seaside resort of Balbec, in Normandy, is where Proust's narrator spends several formative months as a teenager. Balbec is based on Cabourg, where Proust himself wrote several sections of the novel in the Grand Hôtel, which still stands on the seafront.

† Proust's narrator comes across a copy of this book in the library of the Duc de Guermantes; it is a book the narrator's mother read to him as a boy. *François the Waif* is a controversial 'country novel' by George Sand in which a foundling falls in love with his own adoptive mother.

Shakespeare seems to have been particularly fond of Italy; some think he travelled there in the 1580s during his so-called 'lost years'. He set fifteen of his plays in Italian cities (and included references to others).

FLORENCE
All's Well That Ends Well

ILLYRIA*
Twelfth Night

MANTUA
Romeo and Juliet

MESSINA
Antony and Cleopatra
Much Ado About Nothing

MILAN
The Two Gentlemen of Verona
(The Tempest)

NAPLES
(The Tempest)

PADUA
(The Merchant of Venice)
The Taming of the Shrew

PALERMO
The Winter's Tale

ROME
Antony and Cleopatra
Coriolanus
Cymbeline
Julius Caesar
Titus Andronicus

SYRACUSE
(The Comedy of Errors)

VENICE
The Merchant of Venice
Othello

VERONA
Romeo and Juliet
The Taming of the Shrew
The Two Gentlemen of Verona

* Illyria – the setting for *Twelfth Night* – was the name of a region on the Adriatic coast, under Venetian control in Shakespeare's time, as it had been since the thirteenth century. *Twelfth Night* has the character of an Italian play and its sources are Italian, but Duke Orsino's fictional capital is unnamed. One possible model is the Republic of Ragusa, now Dubrovnik, which was then a wealthy, independent city state with a ruling duke.

MISS FLITE'S BIRDS

Miss Flite is a 'crazy old lady', who lodges in a garret of Krook's Rag and Bottle Warehouse in *Bleak House* by Charles Dickens. She was once a ward of chancery, with youth and hope, but was ruined by an interminable lawsuit. Her room is full of caged birds, whose names chart her descent into delusion. She plans to release them on 'the Day of Judgment'.

Hope • Joy • Youth • Peace • Rest • Life • Dust • Ashes • Waste • Want
Ruin • Despair • Madness • Death • Cunning • Folly • Words • Wigs • Rags
Sheepskin • Plunder • Precedent • Jargon • Gammon • Spinach

Some USEFUL WORDS

abibliophobia	English	the fear of running out of reading material
bibliobibuli	English	a person who overindulges in reading
bibliosmia	English	the smell of a good book*
déjà lu	French	the disconcerting feeling that you are reading something for the second time
elucubration	English	reading or writing by candlelight
helluo librorum	Latin	a person with an insatiable appetite for books
lethologica	English	the experience of not being able to remember the right word
librocubicularist	English	a person who reads in bed
mặc khách	Vietnamese	a person who appreciates the beauty of literature
nefelibata	Portuguese	a person with their head in the clouds
scripturient	English	having a passionate urge to write
sesquipedalianists	English	writers with a tendency to use long words
tsundoku	Japanese	the habit of buying more books than you can read
vade mecum	Latin	a book that is always kept to hand

* This word was coined in 2014 by Oliver Tearle, author of *The Secret Library*.

FINNEGANS THUNDER WORDS

Finnegans Wake by James Joyce contains ten 'thunder words', each of which has 100 letters, except the last, which is 101 letters long, so in total they contain 1,001 letters. In *The Bell Jar*, Sylvia Plath describes an attempt to pronounce the first thunder word: 'It sounded like a heavy wooden object falling downstairs, boomp boomp boomp, step after step.'

bababadalgharaghtakamminarronnkonnbronntonnerronntuonnthunntrovarrhounawnskawntoohoohoordenenthurnuk[1]

perkodhuskurunbarggruauyagokgorlayorgromgremmitghundhurthrumathunaradidillifaititillibumullunukkunun[2]

klikkaklakkaklaskaklopatzklatschabattacreppycrottygraddaghsemmihsammihnouithappluddyappladdypkonpkot[3]

bladyughfoulmoecklenburgwhurawhorascortastrumpaporanenrykocksapastippatappatupperstrippuckputtanach[4]

thingcrooklyexineverypasturesixdixlikencehimaroundhersthemaggerbykinkinkankanwithdownmindlookingated[5]

lukkedoerendunandurraskewdylooshoofermoyportertooryzooysphalnabortansporthaokansakroidverjkapakkapuk[6]

bothallchoractorschumminaroundgansumuminarumdrumstrumtruminahumptadumpwaultopoofoolooderamaunsturnup[7]

pappappapparrassannuaragheallachnatullaghmonganmacmacmacwhackfalltherdebblenonthedubblandaddydoodled[8]

husstenhasstencaffincoffintussemtossemdamandamnacosaghcusaghhobixhatouxpeswchbechoscashlcarcarcaract[9]

ullhodturdenweirmudgaardgringnirurdrmolnirfenrirlukkilokkibaugimandodrrerinsurtkrinmgernrackinarockar[10]

1. thunder   2. thunder   3. applause   4. abuse   5. dancing   6. door slamming   7. falling   8. the full name of Persse O'Reilly   9. coughing   10. Norse gods

15

CATS

Percy Bysshe Shelley was not a cat person; he once tied a tomcat to a kite and flew it in a thunderstorm, hoping to see it electrocuted. His earliest surviving poem, written at the age of eleven, is called 'A Cat in Distress'. Shelley's fascination with electricity and lightning may have informed the character of Victor Frankenstein in his wife's famous novel.

Adorno	Julio Cortázar
Bambino	Mark Twain
Beppo	Jorge Luis Borges
Black Madonna	Doris Lessing
Bob*	Charles Dickens
Catarina	Edgar Allan Poe
Cigarette	Albert Camus
Flumbo	Barbara Cartland
Foss†	Edward Lear
Frodo	Robert Penn Warren
General Butchkin	Iris Murdoch
Grimalkin	Christina Rossetti
Hodge	Samuel Johnson
Howl	Allen Ginsberg
Jellylorum	T. S. Eliot
Jeoffry	Christopher Smart
Kafka	Haruki Murakami
Limbo	Aldous Huxley
Magnificat	Philip K. Dick
Marigay (aka Butch)	William S. Burroughs
Pangur	W. H. Auden
Psipsina	Tove Jansson
Rien	Jean-Paul Sartre
Rumpel‡	Robert Southey
Scratchaway	Thomas Hood
Snow White§	Ernest Hemingway
Spider‖	Patricia Highsmith
Taki	Raymond Chandler
Zuleika	Théophile Gautier
Zwerg	Colette

* When Bob died, Dickens had his paw stuffed and mounted on an ivory letter opener.

† Short for Adelphos ('brother'). Half of Foss's tail was missing.

‡ Also known as 'the Most Noble the Archduke Rumpelstiltzchen, Marquis Macbum, Earl Tomlemagne, Baron Raticide, Waowhler, and Skaratch'.

§ Snow White had six toes on each of its front paws and was given to Hemingway by a ship's captain. Today the Ernest Hemingway Home and Museum is home to about sixty six-toed cats.

‖ Highsmith gave Spider to Muriel Spark when the former moved from Italy to Suffolk. 'You could tell he had been a writer's cat,' said Spark. 'He would sit by me, seriously, as I wrote, while all my other cats filtered away.'

'Has a single good author ever owned a dog?' asks Karl Ove Knausgaard in *The New Yorker*. 'Hamsun didn't have a dog. Tor Ulven didn't have a dog. Did Duras have one? I find that hard to imagine. Ibsen, did he have a dog? No. Faulkner? I believe he did. In that case, perhaps his position in the literary canon ought to be reconsidered?'

Baron	Victor Hugo
Basket	Gertrude Stein
Bluebell	Jilly Cooper
Boatswain*	Lord Byron
Bouillabaisse†	Zelda Fitzgerald
Bounce	Alexander Pope
Bromine‡	Anton Chekhov
Chopper	Roald Dahl
Cliché	Dorothy Parker
Daisy	E. B. White
Flush	Elizabeth Barrett Browning
Jeeves	David Foster Wallace
Jofi	Sigmund Freud
Keeper	Emily Brontë
Linky	Edith Wharton
Luath	J. M. Barrie
Marx	George Orwell
Mr Papworth	C. S. Lewis
Pepper	William Wordsworth
Pinka	Virginia Woolf
Possum	Jack London
Pumpkin	Kurt Vonnegut
Roy	Arthur Conan Doyle
Stormy	William Carlos Williams
Tibo	Norman Mailer
Toby§	John Steinbeck
Tosca	Henry James
Typo	Anne Fadiman
Ulisses	Clarice Lispector
Wessex‖	Thomas Hardy

* So attached was Byron to his Newfoundland that when Boatswain died, the poet installed a stone memorial in the grounds of his estate, Newstead Abbey. It is larger than his own gravestone.

† Also known as Muddy Water or Jerry.

‡ The grandson of Bromine, named Box II, was owned by Vladimir Nabokov.

§ Toby ate half of the draft of *Of Mice and Men*. 'My setter pup, left alone one night, made confetti of about half of my book,' Steinbeck wrote. 'Two months work to do over again. It sets me back. There was no other draft. I was pretty mad but the poor little fellow may have been acting critically.' He later appointed Toby 'lieutenant-colonel in charge of literature'.

‖ Hardy also had cats named Cobby and Trot, short for 'Kiddleywinkempoops'.

The FOOTNOTE MARKERS

The first editorial mark was the *obeliskos* ('little roasting spit'), which was used in 280 BC by Zenodotus of Ephesus, the librarian of Alexandria, to mark spurious lines in faulty translations of Homer. The *asteriskos* ('little star') was introduced eighty years later by Aristophanes of Byzantium, another librarian, to mark duplicate lines, and these and other marks were codified during the second century BC by Aristarchus of Samothrace, yet another librarian. Modern versions of these symbols are used as footnote markers, usually in the order below, although today typographers tend to use numbers if there are more than three notes to a page.

| the asterisk, or star | the obelisk, or dagger | the diesis, or double dagger | the silcrow, or section sign | the pipe, or caesura mark | the pilcrow, or paragraph mark |

The ALPHABET MYSTERIES

In 1982, the US author Sue Grafton published the first Kinsey Millhone mystery, *A is for Alibi*. She went on to publish twenty-four alphabetically titled sequels but died before she was able to write *Z is for Zero*. Her heirs have not sanctioned another writer to complete the project, stating that 'as far as we in the family are concerned, the alphabet now ends at Y'.

A is for Alibi · B is for Burglar · C is for Corpse · D is for Deadbeat
E is for Evidence · F is for Fugitive · G is for Gumshoe
H is for Homicide · I is for Innocent · J is for Judgment
K is for Killer · L is for Lawless · M is for Malice · N is for Noose
O is for Outlaw · P is for Peril · Q is for Quarry · R is for Ricochet
S is for Silence · T is for Trespass · U is for Undertow
V is for Vengeance · W is for Wasted · X* · Y is for Yesterday

* Grafton struggled with this title. It 'almost has to be Xenophobe or Xenophobia', she said in 2013. 'I've checked the penal codes in most states and xylophone isn't a crime, so I'm stuck.' In the end, she published the novel under the single-letter title *X* (see p.118).

REMEDIES *for* LOW SPIRITS

The clergyman and essayist Sydney Smith is best remembered for his witty letters and a rhyming recipe for anchovy salad. He wrote to his friend, Lady Georgiana Morpeth, on hearing that she was suffering from depression:

Foston, Feb. 16th, 1820

Dear Lady Georgiana, –

Nobody has suffered more from low spirits than I have done – so I feel for you.

1st.   Live as well as you dare.

2nd.   Go into the shower-bath with a small quantity of water at a temperature low enough to give you a slight sensation of cold, 75° or 80°.

3rd.   Amusing books.

4th.   Short views of human life – not further than dinner or tea.

5th.   Be as busy as you can.

6th.   See as much as you can of those friends who like and respect you.

7th.   And of those acquaintances who amuse you.

8th.   Make no secret of low spirits to your friends, but talk of them freely – they are always worse for dignified concealment.

9th.   Attend to the effects tea and coffee produce upon you.

10th.   Compare your lot with that of other people.

11th.   Don't expect too much from human life – a sorry business at the best.

12th.   Avoid poetry, dramatic representations (except comedy), music, serious novels, melancholy sentimental people, and every thing likely to excite feeling or emotion not ending in active benevolence.

13th.   *Do good*, and endeavour to please everybody of every degree.

14th.   Be as much as you can in the open air without fatigue.

15th.   Make the room where you commonly sit, gay and pleasant.

16th.   Struggle little by little against idleness.

17th.   Don't be too severe upon yourself, or underrate yourself, but do yourself justice.

18th.   Keep good blazing fires.

19th.   Be firm and constant in the exercise of rational religion.

20th.   Believe me, dear Lady Georgiana,

Very truly yours, Sydney Smith

Some VERY SHORT STORIES

Ernest Hemingway is said to have bet $10, during lunch at the Algonquin Hotel in New York, that he could tell a satisfying short story in just six words. He wrote on a napkin: 'For sale: baby shoes, never worn.' It's a good myth, though almost certainly untrue. Nevertheless, 'flash fiction' competitions have since become popular; categories include the 'six-word story', the 'dribble' (fifty words) and the 'drabble' (100 words).

I kept myself alive. — 'Widow's First Year' by Joyce Carol Oates

Longed for him. Got him. Shit. — Margaret Atwood

TIME MACHINE REACHES FUTURE!!! ... nobody there ...
    — Harry Harrison

Easy. Just touch the match to — Ursula K. Le Guin

Machine. Unexpectedly, I'd invented a time — Alan Moore

Aliens disguised as typewriters? I've never heard such
    — Colin Greenland

God said, 'Cancel Program GENESIS.' The universe ceased to exist.
    — Arthur C. Clarke

The stranger climbed the stairs in the dark: tick-tock, tick-tock, tick-tock. — Jorge Luis Borges & Adolfo Bioy Casares

The PRINCES of HELL

'Better to reign in Hell,' declares Satan, in Milton's *Paradise Lost*, 'than serve in Heav'n.' Satan rules Hell from his capital city of Pandaemonium, where he holds his 'Stygian Counsel' with twelve demonic princes.

Beelzebub* • Moloch • Chemos • Baal • Astarte • Thammuz
Dagon • Rimmon • Osiris • Isis • Orus • Belial

---

* Beelzebub is Satan's second-in-command, his 'bold Compeer'. His name means 'Lord of the Flies'.

The MOONS of URANUS

The planet Uranus has five major moons, named after characters from Shakespeare and Alexander Pope's *The Rape of the Lock*: Titania and Oberon were discovered by William Herschel in 1787, Ariel and Umbriel in 1851 by William Lassell, and Miranda by Gerard Kuiper in 1948. Uranus also has twenty-two smaller moons, named after more Shakespearean characters.

Miranda (*⅛ the size of our moon*)	Craters named after characters from Shakespeare's *The Tempest*	Alonso · Ferdinand · Francisco Gonzalo · Prospero · Stephano Trinculo
Ariel (*⅓ the size of our moon*)	Craters named after bright spirits from various mythologies	Abans · Agape* · Ataksak Befana · Berylune · Deive · Djadek Domovoy · Finvara · Gwyn Huon† · Laica · Mab‡ · Melusine Oonagh · Rima§ · Yangoor
Umbriel (*⅓ the size of our moon*)	Craters named after dark spirits from various mythologies	Alberich‖ · Fin · Gob · Kanaloa Malingee · Minepa · Peri Setebos¶ · Skynd · Vuver Wokolo · Wunda · Zlyden
Titania (*½ the size of our moon*)	Craters named after female characters from Shakespeare	Adriana · Bona · Calpurnia Elinor · Gertrude · Imogen Iras · Jessica · Katherine · Lucetta Marina · Mopsa · Phrynia Ursula · Valeria
Oberon (*½ the size of our moon*)	Craters named after male characters from Shakespeare	Antony · Caesar · Coriolanus Falstaff · Hamlet · Lear Macbeth · Othello · Romeo

* Agape is a fairy character in *The Faerie Queene* by Edmund Spenser.
† Huon succeeds Oberon as King of the Fairies in the thirteenth-century *Huon of Bordeaux*.
‡ Mab is mentioned as Queen of the Fairies in Shakespeare's *Romeo and Juliet*.
§ Rima is a 'bird girl' in *Green Mansions* by William Henry Hudson.
‖ Alberich is a dwarf who guards the Nibelung gold in the *Nibelungenlied*; 'Alberich' is the German equivalent of the name 'Oberon'.
¶ Setebos is Caliban's god in Shakespeare's *The Tempest*.

From A to B

'You never dedicate a book to another writer,' said William Gaddis. 'You'd worry that he wouldn't like it.' Even so, the following works were dedicated by their authors to other authors, as a token – in most cases – of respect:

Lucky Jim	Kingsley Amis	Philip Larkin
London Fields	Martin Amis	Kingsley Amis
Jane Eyre	Charlotte Brontë	William Makepeace Thackeray
Music for Chameleons	Truman Capote	Tennessee Williams
O Pioneers!	Willa Cather	Sarah Orne Jewett
Troilus and Criseyde	Geoffrey Chaucer	John Gower
Halloween Party	Agatha Christie	P. G. Wodehouse
The Secret Agent	Joseph Conrad	H. G. Wells
The Waste Land	T. S. Eliot	Ezra Pound
In Praise of Folly	Erasmus	Thomas More
The Great Gatsby	F. Scott Fitzgerald	Zelda Fitzgerald
A Modern Comedy	John Galsworthy	Max Beerbohm
She Stoops to Conquer	Oliver Goldsmith	Samuel Johnson
The Screwtape Letters	C. S. Lewis	J. R. R. Tolkien
Babbitt	Sinclair Lewis	Edith Wharton
Moby-Dick	Herman Melville	Nathaniel Hawthorne
Ladders to Fire	Anaïs Nin	Gore Vidal
Twelve Years a Slave	Solomon Northup	Harriet Beecher Stowe
Olivia	Olivia (see p.65)	Virginia Woolf
Life A User's Manual	Georges Perec	Raymond Queneau
Gravity's Rainbow	Thomas Pynchon	Richard Fariña
The Little Prince	Antoine de Saint-Exupéry	Léon Werth
Nausea	Jean-Paul Sartre	'The Beaver'*
Under the Sign of Saturn	Susan Sontag	Joseph Brodsky
The Cutting of the Forest	Leo Tolstoy	Ivan Turgenev
The Song of Triumphant Love	Ivan Turgenev	Gustave Flaubert
The Loved One	Evelyn Waugh	Nancy Mitford
The Prelude	William Wordsworth	Samuel Taylor Coleridge

* This was Sartre's pet name for Simone de Beauvoir, his lifelong 'soul partner'.

Some BIOGRAPHICAL PICTURES

Some writers are fiercely private; others lead flamboyant lives. Whatever the case, readers are intrigued by the human reality behind great fiction, which may explain why there are so many films about authors' lives.

Capote	Philip Seymour Hoffman	*as*	Truman Capote
Colette	Keira Knightley	*as*	Colette
Enid	Helena Bonham Carter	*as*	Enid Blyton
Iris	Judi Dench	*as*	Iris Murdoch
Kafka	Jeremy Irons	*as*	Franz Kafka
Shirley	Elisabeth Moss	*as*	Shirley Jackson
Sylvia	Gwyneth Paltrow	*as*	Sylvia Plath
Wilde	Stephen Fry	*as*	Oscar Wilde

The SEVEN DWARFS

In the fairy tale *Schneewittchen*, the Brothers Grimm tell how Snow White shelters in a cottage with seven dwarfs; the dwarfs' names are not given, however, so subsequent adaptations have had to supply their own.

Snow White and the Seven Dwarfs (1912 Broadway play)
Blick · Flick · Glick · Snick · Plick · Whick · Quee

Snow White and the Seven Dwarfs (1937 Disney film)
Doc · Grumpy · Happy · Sleepy · Bashful · Sneezy · Dopey*

Schneewittchen (2009 German TV film)
Gorm · Knirps · Niffel · Quarx · Querx · Schrat · Wichtel

Snow White and the Huntsman (2012 feature film)
Beith · Muir · Quert · Coll · Duir · Gort · Nion · Gus†

---

* Other names that Disney considered include Awful, Biggy, Chesty, Dirty, Flabby, Gloomy, Hotsy, Jumpy, Lazy, Nifty, Puffy, Shifty, Thrifty and Wistful.

† Initially there are eight dwarfs in this adaptation, all named after letters of the Ogham alphabet (see p.94) except Gus, the youngest, who sacrifices his life to save Snow White.

The NYCTOGRAPHIC SQUARE ALPHABET

a	b	c	d	e	f	g

h	i	j	k	l	m	n

o	p	q	r	s	t	u

v	w	x	y	z

Like the White Knight in *Through the Looking-Glass*, Lewis Carroll was a keen inventor: he devised a postage-stamp case, a steering mechanism for tricycles, a travel chess set and 'the Nyctograph', a device for recording one's thoughts in the dark. This last invention consisted of a small piece of pasteboard with quarter-inch squares cut out, which one could place inside a notebook and fill with letters in a 'square alphabet' of Carroll's own invention. He explained in a letter to the *Lady* magazine in 1891:

> Any one who has tried, as I have often done, the process of getting out of bed at 2 a.m. in a winter night, lighting a candle, and recording some happy thought which would probably be otherwise forgotten, will agree with me it entails much discomfort. All I have now to do, if I wake and think of something I wish to record, is to draw from under the pillow a small memorandum book containing my Nyctograph, write a few lines, or even a few pages, without even putting the hands outside the bed-clothes, replace the book, and go to sleep again.

In 2011, the US publisher Evertype released an edition of Carroll's *Alice's Adventures in Wonderland*, printed in the Nyctographic Square Alphabet.

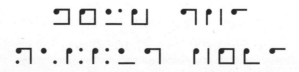

The SEVEN DEADLY SINS

The seven deadly sins were settled by Pope Gregory the Great in 590 and became a key notion of medieval Christianity. In the poem *Piers Plowman* by William Langland, they are personified as grotesque characters:

> ENVY was as pale as a pelet, in the palsy he semed, / And clothed in a kaurymaury. ¶ GLUTTONY pissed a potel in a Paternoster-while, / And blew his rounde ruwet at his ruggebones ende. ¶ GREED was bitelbrowed and baberlipped, with two blered eighen, / And as a letheren purs lolled hise chekes. ¶ LUST seide 'Allas!' and on Oure Lady he cryde. ¶ PRIDE platte hire to the erthe / And lay longe er she loked. ¶ SLOTH [was] al bislabered, with two slymed eighen. ¶ WRATH with two white eighen, / And nevelynge with the nose, and his nekke hangyng.

The DIET of a NATURALIST

Charles Darwin was a member of a dining society at Cambridge University which experimented with eating 'strange flesh'. They consumed bitterns, owls and various other 'birds and beasts which were before unknown to human palate'. His culinary researches continued when, as a 22-year-old amateur naturalist, he joined Captain FitzRoy's round-the-world expedition; here are some extracts from his diary, published as *The Voyage of the Beagle*:

Agouti	'the very best meat I ever tasted'
Armadillo	'a most excellent dish when roasted in its shell'
Capybara	'the meat is very indifferent'
Catfish	'good eating'
Iguana	'a white meat, which is liked by those whose stomachs soar above all prejudices'
Puma	'remarkably like veal in taste'
Tortoise, Giant	'the breast-plate roasted (as the Gauchos do carne con cuero), with the flesh on it, is very good; and the young tortoises make excellent soup'

A LIST *of* TROUBLES

From 1932, F. Scott Fitzgerald assembled notebooks, organizing them under alphabetical headings such as (A) for Anecdotes; (C) for Conversation and Things Overheard; (F) for Feelings & Emotions (without girls); (G) for Descriptions of Girls; and (R) for Rough Stuff. In 1935, under (K) for Karacters, he added the following sorry 'List of Troubles':

heart burn · eczema · piles · flu · night sweats · alcoholism
infected nose · insomnia · ruined nerves · chronic cough
aching teeth · shortness of breath · falling hair · cramps in feet
tingling feet · constipation · cirrhosis of the liver
stomach ulcers · depression and melancholia

The FELLOWSHIP *of* PILGRIMS

Geoffrey Chaucer never finished *The Canterbury Tales*. In the prologue, the narrator counts twenty-nine fellow pilgrims, who decide to ride together from Southwark to Canterbury, telling stories along the way. The host suggests they tell two tales each on the way there and two on the way back, but in the text that survives, only twenty-three pilgrims tell tales.

THE TALE TELLERS
The Knight · The Miller (Robin) · The Reeve (Oswald)
The Cook (Roger) · The Man of Law · The Wife of Bath (Alison)
The Friar (Hubert) · The Summoner · The Clerk · The Merchant
The Squire · The Franklin · The Physician · The Pardoner
The Shipman · The Prioress (Eglentine) · The Narrator (Chaucer)
The Monk (Piers) · The Nun's Priest (John) · The Second Nun
The Canon's Yeoman* · The Manciple · The Parson

THE OTHER PILGRIMS
The Host (Harry Bailly) · The Knight's Yeoman · The Second Priest
The Third Priest · The Five Guildsmen (Haberdasher, Carpenter, Weaver, Dyer and Tapestry-Maker) · The Ploughman · The Canon*

* The Canon and the Canon's Yeoman are not part of the original party leaving from Southwark. They meet the group at the village of Boughton under Blean, five miles outside Canterbury.

Some ALTERNATIVE TITLES

Authors occasionally let us choose what to call their books. Alternative titles – unlike subtitles (see p.140) – are separated by an 'or' which appears to give both titles equal weight, although, in practice, second titles are rarely used in preference to first titles. One exception is Captain Frederick Marryat's *Snarleyyow, or, The Dog Fiend*, which is usually referred to simply as *The Dog Fiend*. Here are some more alternative titles:

Euphues or *The Anatomy of Wit*		John Lyly
Guy Mannering or *The Astrologer*		Walter Scott
An Apprenticeship or *The Book of Pleasures*		Clarice Lispector (see also p.51)
Slaughterhouse-Five or *The Children's Crusade: A Duty-Dance with Death*		Kurt Vonnegut
Blood Meridian or *The Evening Redness in the West*		Cormac McCarthy
Twilight of the Idols or *How to Philosophize with a Hammer*		Friedrich Nietzsche
Uncle Tom's Cabin or *Life Among the Lowly*		Harriet Beecher Stowe
Lolly Willowes or *The Loving Huntsman*		Sylvia Townsend Warner
She Stoops to Conquer or *The Mistakes of a Night*		Oliver Goldsmith
Frankenstein or *The Modern Prometheus*		Mary Shelley
Treasure Island or *The Mutiny on the Hispaniola*		Robert Louis Stevenson
Oliver Twist or *The Parish Boy's Progress*		Charles Dickens
Candide or *Optimism*		Voltaire
Erewhon or *Over the Range*		Samuel Butler
Zuleika Dobson or *An Oxford Love Story*		Max Beerbohm
Cakes and Ale or *The Skeleton in the Cupboard*		W. Somerset Maugham
The Hobbit or *There and Back Again*		J. R. R. Tolkien
Pamela or *Virtue Rewarded*		Samuel Richardson
Kubla Khan or *A Vision in a Dream: A Fragment*		Samuel Taylor Coleridge
Moby-Dick or *The Whale*		Herman Melville
Twelfth Night or *What You Will*		William Shakespeare

DICTIONARY CORNER

Samuel Johnson slipped humorous definitions into his 1755 *Dictionary of the English Language*;* Gustave Flaubert spent years working on a *Dictionary of Received Ideas*, a satirical guide to the platitudes and foibles of nineteenth-century France;† and another literary lexicographer was Ambrose Bierce, whose scabrous *Devil's Dictionary* definitions‡ appeared in the San Francisco *Wasp* magazine in the late nineteenth century. Here are some selected definitions from these three literary lexicons:

	JOHNSON	FLAUBERT	BIERCE
Air	The element encompassing the terraqueous globe.	Always beware of fresh air.	A nutritious substance supplied by a bountiful Providence for the fattening of the poor.
Art	The power of doing something not taught by nature and instinct.	Leads to the workhouse.	This word has no definition.
Back	The hinder part of the body, from the neck to the thighs.	A slap on the back can give you tuberculosis.	That part of your friend which it is your privilege to contemplate in your adversity.
Cat	A domestick animal that catches mice.	Are treacherous. Call them 'drawing-room tigers'.	A soft, indestructible automaton provided by nature to be kicked when things go wrong in the domestic circle.
Child	An infant, or very young person.	Display a lyrical fondness for them when there are people present.	An accident to the occurrence of which all the forces and arrangements of nature are specifically devised.
Critic	A man skilled in the art of judging of literature.	Supposed to know everything, to have read everything, to have seen everything.	A person who boasts himself hard to please because nobody tries to please him.
Dictionary	A book containing the words of any language.	Say of it: 'It's only for ignoramuses!'	A malevolent literary device for cramping the growth of a language and making it hard and inelastic.§

28

Idler	A lazy person; a sluggard.	All Parisians are idlers.	A model farm where the devil experiments with seeds of new sins and promotes the growth of staple vices.
Laughter	Convulsive merriment.	Always 'Homeric'.	An interior convulsion, producing a distortion of the features and accompanied by inarticulate noises.
Lawyer	Professor of law; advocate; pleader.	Too many of them in Parliament.	One skilled in circumvention of the law.
Medicine	Physick; any remedy administered by a physician.	When in good health, make fun of it.	A stone flung down the Bowery to kill a dog in Broadway.
Novel	A small tale, generally of love.	Corrupts the masses.	A short story padded.
Oyster	A bivalve testaceous fish.	Nobody eats them any more: they are really far too dear!	A slimy, gobby shellfish which civilization gives men the hardihood to eat without removing its entrails.
Philosophy	Knowledge natural or moral.	Always snigger at it.	A route of many roads leading from nowhere to nothing.
Poetry	Metrical composition.	Completely useless and out of date.	A form of expression peculiar to the Land beyond the Magazines.
Wit	The powers of the mind; the mental faculties.	Always preceded by 'sparkling'.	The salt with which the American humorist spoils his intellectual cookery by leaving it out.
Youth	The part of life succeeding to childhood and adolescence.	What a wonderful thing it is!	The Period of Possibility.

* Such as: 'Lexicographer: A writer of dictionaries; a harmless drudge.'
† Of 'spelling', Flaubert writes: 'Like mathematics. Not necessary if you have style.'
‡ Bierce defined a 'piano' as 'a parlor utensil for subduing the impenitent visitor. It is operated by depressing the keys of the machine and the spirits of the audience.'
§ 'This dictionary, however, is a most useful work,' clarifies its fictional author Dr John Satan.

The CLASSIC CHINESE NOVELS

Traditionally, four novels are considered the masterpieces of Chinese literature. They are the most studied and most imitated works of Chinese prose fiction and serve as cultural touchstones today in the way that the works of Dante, Shakespeare and Cervantes do in the west. All four combine historical narratives with elements of romance and folklore and are written in a blend of classical and vernacular Chinese.

The Romance of the Three Kingdoms attributed to Luo Guanzhong
Fourteenth century
> Feudal warlords battle for power in the final years of the Han Dynasty; the book features almost a thousand characters.

The Water Margin or *Outlaws of the Marsh* attributed to Shi Nai'an
Fourteenth century
> A hundred outlaws gather at the Liangshan Marsh. They fight against the Song emperor and then for him against Liao rebels.

The Journey to the West or *Monkey* attributed to Wu Ch'eng-en
Sixteenth century
> A Buddhist monk travels to India seeking a sacred text, with magical animal sidekicks: Pig, Sandy and the Monkey King.

The Dream of the Red Chamber or *The Story of the Stone* by Cao Xueqin
Eighteenth century
> A young man loves one cousin but is betrothed to another. As his family's fortunes fluctuate, he finally achieves enlightenment.

Sometimes the list is extended to include:

The Plum in the Golden Vase or *The Golden Lotus* attributed to 'The Scoffing Scholar of Lanling'
Sixteenth century
> In this erotic spin-off from *The Water Margin*, a merchant has sex with six wives, twelve mistresses and a male servant.

The Unofficial History of the Scholars or *The Scholars* by Wu Jingzi
Eighteenth century
> A compendium of stories which satirizes ambitious academics of the Ming Dynasty and celebrates the ideals of Confucianism.

The SEVEN COMMANDMENTS *of* ANIMALISM

In *Animal Farm* by George Orwell, the animals of Manor Farm in Sussex overthrow their drunken human farmer. The pigs then paint the seven 'unalterable' commandments of the new Animalist government on the wall of the big barn, in white letters that can be read thirty yards away.

Whatever goes upon two legs is an enemy.
Whatever goes upon four legs, or has wings, is a friend.
No animal shall wear clothes.
No animal shall sleep in a bed.
No animal shall drink alcohol.
No animal shall kill any other animal.
All animals are equal.

In the months that follow, the other animals occasionally question their own memories as certain commandments are silently amended:

No animal shall sleep in a bed *with sheets*.
No animal shall drink alcohol *to excess*.
No animal shall kill any other animal *without cause*.

And then one day, when Clover the carthorse asks Benjamin the donkey to read what's on the wall, there is nothing except a single commandment:

ALL ANIMALS ARE EQUAL
BUT SOME ANIMALS ARE MORE EQUAL THAN OTHERS.

THREE MEN *in a* BOAT

George • Harris • J.

The novel *Three Men in a Boat* by Jerome K. Jerome was based on Thames boating trips that Jerome made with his friends George Wingrave (George) and Carl Hentschel (Harris). The book's subtitle, *To Say Nothing of the Dog*, refers to J.'s spirited (and fictional) fox terrier, Montmorency. The friends were reunited in a sequel, *Three Men on the Bummel*, in which they make a tour of Germany on a bicycle and a tandem.

Some BOOKS that were WRITTEN QUICKLY

Barbara Cartland wrote 723 novels over a period of seventy-six years and is said to hold the Guinness World Record for the most books published in a year (twenty-three in 1983, including *The Unwanted Wedding* and *Lights, Laughter and a Lady*). Here are some other books that were written quickly:

25 hours
154 pages
The Dancer at the Gai-Moulin by Georges Simenon (who frequently wrote 80 pages before breakfast)

2½ days
216 pages
The Boy in the Striped Pyjamas by John Boyne (who had the idea on Tuesday 27 April 2004, and wrote nonstop until noon on Friday)

3 days
68 pages
The Strange Case of Dr Jekyll and Mr Hyde by Robert Louis Stevenson (who dreamed that little 'Brownies' gave him the plot)

4 days
120 pages
Goodbye, Mr Chips by James Hilton (who conceived the book during a bicycle ride to 'clear his head')

1 week
110 pages
The History of Rasselas, Prince of Abissinia by Samuel Johnson (who wrote it to pay the costs of his mother's funeral)

2 weeks
158 pages
The Alchemist by Paulo Coelho (who said, 'The book was already written in my soul')

3 weeks
140 pages
A Clockwork Orange by Anthony Burgess (who described it as a '*jeu d'esprit* knocked off for money')

3 weeks
136 pages
Les Enfants Terribles by Jean Cocteau (who wrote it while weaning himself off an opium addiction)

3 weeks
128 pages
A Study in Scarlet by Arthur Conan Doyle (who wrote it while working as a GP in Hampshire)

3 weeks
270 pages
The Tortoise and the Hare by Elizabeth Jenkins (who never looked at the text again)

4 weeks
224 pages
The Gambler by Fyodor Dostoyevsky (who wrote it to pay off pressing gambling debts)

4 weeks
264 pages
The Remains of the Day by Kazuo Ishiguro (who wrote it on a 'crash' schedule of 10½-hour days, six days a week)

The WIZARDS of MIDDLE-EARTH

In J. R. R. Tolkien's world of Middle-earth, there are five guardian spirits who take the form of elderly men. They are known as 'Wizards' by Hobbits and Men, and as 'the Istari' by the Elves; they are assigned different colours.

Saruman the White, later Saruman of Many Colours
Gandalf the Grey, later Gandalf the White · Radagast the Brown
Alatar the Blue · Pallando the Blue

The BIRDS of SHAKESPEARE

In 1890, the ornithologist Eugene Schieffelin released sixty European starlings in New York's Central Park. Schieffelin was the chairman of the American Acclimatization Society, dedicated to introducing non-native species to North America. This came with unintended consequences: the US is now home to 200 million starlings, belligerent birds that fly in dense flocks, eat grain intended for livestock and pose a danger to aeroplanes. It is said that Schieffelin released the starlings because he wished to introduce all the birds mentioned in the plays of Shakespeare to North America. If this is true, he would have needed to tick off the following sixty species:

barnacle (*barnacle goose*) · bunting · buzzard · chough · cock · cormorant
crow · cuckoo · daw (*jackdaw*) · dive-dapper (*little grebe*) · dove · duck
eagle · estridge (*goshawk*) · eyas-musket (*young male sparrowhawk*) · falcon
finch · goose · guinea hen · gull · halcyon (*kingfisher*) · hawk · hedge-
sparrow (*dunnock*) · jay · kite · lapwing · lark · loon (*great crested grebe*)
martlet (*house martin*) · nightingale · night-raven (*nightjar*) · osprey · ostrich
ousel (*blackbird*) · owl · parrot · partridge · peacock · pelican · pheasant
pie (*magpie*) · pigeon · quail · raven · rook · ruddock (*robin*) · scamel
(*bermuda petrel*) · snipe · sparrow · staniel (*kestrel*) · starling* · swallow
swan · tercel (*male peregrine*) · throstel (*thrush*) · turkey · vulture
(*white-tailed eagle*) · wagtail · woodcock · wren

---

* Shakespeare's only reference to starlings is in *Henry IV, Part 1*. The rebel Hotspur, referring to the king and his enemy Mortimer, cries: 'Nay, I'll have a starling shall be taught to speak / Nothing but "Mortimer", and give it him / To keep his anger still in motion.'

The INFAMOUS BIBLES

Since the King James Version of the Bible was first published in 1611, it has gone through many different editions. Some notorious printings have included accidental typesetting errors, after which they have been named.

The 'Printers Bible'	1612	'printers have persecuted me without a cause' *Psalm* 119:161 (instead of 'princes')
The 'Wicked Bible'	1631	'Thou shalt commit adultery' *Exodus* 20:14 (instead of 'shalt not')
The 'More Sea Bible'	1641	'and there was more sea' *Revelation* 21:1 (instead of 'no more sea')
The 'Buggre Alle This Bible'*	1651	'Buggre Alle this for a Larke. I amme sick to mye Hart of typeſettinge' *Ezekiel* 48:5 [replaced]
The 'Unrighteous Bible'	1653	'the unrighteous shall inherit the kingdom of God' *1 Corinthians* 6:9 (instead of 'shall not')
The 'Sinner's Bible'	1716	'sin on more' *Jeremiah* 31:34 (instead of 'sin no more')
The 'Vinegar Bible'	1717	'The Parable of the Vinegar' *Luke* 20 (instead of 'Vineyard')
The 'Fool's Bible'	1763	'the fool hath said in his heart, There is a God' *Psalm* 14:1 (instead of 'no God')
The 'Murderers Bible'	1801	'These are murderers, complainers' *Jude* 16 (instead of 'murmurers')
The 'Lions Bible'	1804	'thy son that shall come forth out of thy lions' *1 Kings* 8:19 (instead of 'loins')
The 'Camels Bible'	1823	'Rebekah arose, and her camels, and they rode upon the camels' *Genesis* 24:61 (instead of 'damsels')
The 'Owls Bible'	1944	'being in subjection to their owl husbands' *1 Peter* 3:5 (instead of 'own')

---

* This is the only fictional Bible on this list. It appears in *Good Omens* by Neil Gaiman and Terry Pratchett, among the Infamous Bible collection of Aziraphale, the angel of the flaming sword. Its name may have been partly inspired by the genuine 'Bug Bible' of 1535, in which Psalm 91:5 reads: 'Thou shall not nede to be afrayed for eny bugges by night.'

The SEVEN BASIC PLOTS

In 2004, Christopher Booker, the founder of *Private Eye* magazine, published *The Seven Basic Plots*, a vast book on which he had been working for more than thirty years. Having studied thousands of stories, from Greek drama and European fairy tales to nineteenth-century novels and modern horror films, he concluded that they all had one of seven archetypal plots.

Overcoming the Monster · Rags to Riches · The Quest
Voyage and Return · Comedy · Tragedy · Rebirth

The HETERONYMS of FERNANDO PESSOA

The Portuguese poet Fernando Pessoa wrote in English, Portuguese and French under an array of 'heteronyms', fully developed fictional characters with distinctive writing styles. His three principal heteronyms were the self-taught genius Alberto Caeiro (1889–1915), author of *The Keeper of Sheep* and *The Shepherd in Love*, and his two protégés, the doctor Ricardo Reis (b. 1887), author of classical odes in the style of Horace, and Álvaro de Campos (b. 1890), a bisexual former naval engineer. 'These individuals should be considered distinct from their author,' wrote Pessoa. 'Each one forms a kind of drama, and all of them together form another drama.' Here is a selection of his other heteronyms:

Charles Robert Anon · Dr Faustino Antunes · I. I. Crosse
Horace James Faber · William Jinks · Maria José
Friar Maurice · Joaquim Moura-Costa · Dr Pancrácio
Pantaleão · the Chevalier de Pas · Fernando Pessoa* · Pip
Alexander Search · Jean Seul de Méluret · Bernardo Soares[†]
Sidney Parkinson Stool · Tagus · the Baron of Teive
Dr Gaudêncio Turnips · Frederick Wyatt

* Pessoa used 'Fernando Pessoa' as both an autonym (his real name) and a heteronym (another fictional pupil of Alberto Caeiro). As he said, 'Fernando Pessoa' is just as much a *fingidor* ('counterfeiter') as the others.
† Soares was a fictional assistant bookkeeper in Lisbon and the author of *The Book of Disquiet*, the fragmentary masterpiece for which Pessoa is perhaps best known.

A RECIPE *for* HELL-BROTH

When the hurlyburly's done, treat yourself to a charmed pot of hell-broth. This foul and fair concoction, brewed on the heath by the weird sisters in Shakespeare's *Macbeth*, will impress evil spirits and Scottish kings alike. Serve with sow's blood and the sweat of a hanged murderer.

INGREDIENTS

toad, venomous · fillet of a fenny snake · eye of newt · toe of frog · wool of bat · tongue of dog · adder's fork · blind-worm's sting · lizard's leg · howlet's wing · scale of dragon · tooth of wolf · witches' mummy · maw and gulf of the salt-sea shark, ravin'd · root of hemlock, digg'd i'th' dark · liver of blaspheming Jew · gall of goat · yew slips, sliver'd in the moon's eclipse · nose of Turk · Tartar's lips · finger of birth-strangled babe, ditch-deliver'd · tiger's chaudron · baboon's blood, for cooling

METHOD

Round about the
cauldron go;
In the poison'd
entrails throw.

For a charm of
powerful trouble,
Like a hell-broth boil
and bubble.

Cool it with a
baboon's blood:
Then the charm is
firm and good.

FIFTEEN MEN *on the* DEAD MAN'S CHEST

'Yo-ho-ho, and a bottle of rum!' sings the old sea-dog at the start of Robert Louis Stevenson's *Treasure Island*. Billy Bones's song likely commemorates his crewmates, who served under Captain Flint on the pirate ship *Walrus*.

Job Anderson · Billy Bones · Black Dog · Ben Gunn
Israel Hands · George Merry · Tom Morgan · Blind Pew
Long John Silver · and six sailors murdered by Flint*

* When Captain Flint buried his treasure chest, he was helped by six seamen, whom he then murdered. Flint dragged one of the sailors, Allardyce, up Spy-Glass Hill and arranged his limbs to point towards the treasure.

The MEANING *of* LIFF

In 1983, Douglas Adams and John Lloyd published *The Meaning of Liff*, a 'dictionary of things there should be words for'. They assigned humorous new meanings to place names, such as Liff, which is a small Scottish village near Dundee.* Here are some of their more bookish entries:

ahenny *adj.*   The way people stand when examining other people's bookshelves.

ballycumber *n.*   One of the six half-read books lying somewhere in your bed.

bathel *vb.*   To pretend to have read the book under discussion when in fact you've only seen the TV series.

beppu *n.*   The triumphant slamming shut of a book after reading the final page.

dalmilling *ptcpl. vb.*   Continually making small talk to someone who is trying to read a book.

fritham *n.*   A paragraph that you get stuck on in a book. The more you read it, the less it means to you.

great tosson *n.*   A fat book containing four words and six cartoons which costs £6.95.

great wakering *ptcpl. vb.*   Panic which sets in when you badly need to go to the lavatory and cannot make up your mind about what book or magazine to take with you.

kentucky *adj.*   Fitting exactly and satisfyingly. [...] The last book which precisely fills a bookshelf is said to fit 'real nice and kentucky'.

nossob *n.*   Any word that looks as if it's probably another word backwards but turns out not to be.

pulverbatch *n.*   The first paragraph of the blurb on a dust-jacket in which famous authors claim to had a series of menial jobs in their youth.

ripon *vb.*   (Of literary critics) To include all the best jokes from the book in the review to make it look as if the critic thought of them.

---

* The first edition had a sticker which read 'THIS BOOK WILL CHANGE YOUR LIFE'. Inside, the definition of 'Liff' was: 'A book, the contents of which are totally belied by its cover. For instance, any book the dust jacket of which bears the words, "This book will change your life."'

The SOT-WEED FACTOR

Ebenezer Cooke was a London lawyer who travelled to the British colony of Maryland in the late seventeenth century and wrote a poem in 1708 called *The Sot-Weed Factor*, a scathing, satirical portrait of America. In 1960, the American novelist John Barth published a novel about Cooke with the same title. Barth's *Sot-Weed Factor* is a bawdy, picaresque, digressive epic, written in the style of Henry Fielding and Laurence Sterne. At one point, two Maryland hookers have a memorable exchange.

'A hooker,' the woman repeated with a wink. 'A *quail*, don't ye know.'

'A quail!' the woman named Grace shrieked. 'You call me a quail, you – you *gaullefretière*!'

'Whore!' shouted the first.

'*Bas-cul!*' retorted the other.

'Frisker!'	'Fastfanny!'	'Coxswain!'	'Vagrant!'
'*Consoeur!*'	'*Gaure!*'	shouted the	'*Postiqueuse!*'
'Trull!'	'Ringer!'	one whose turn	'Arsebender!'
'*Friquenelle!*'	'*Bringue!*'	it was to play.	'*Tireuse de vinaigre!*'
'Sow!'	'Capercock!'	'*Trottière!*'	'Sally-dally!'
'*Usagère!*'	'*Ancelle!*'	Grace replied.	'*Rigobette!*'
'Bawd!'	'Nellie!'	'Conycatcher!'	'Bitch!'
'*Viagère!*'	'*Gallière!*'	'*Gourgandine!*'	'*Prêtresse du*
'Strawgirl!'	'Chubcheeker!'	'Tart!'	*membre!*'
'*Sérane!*'	'*Chèvre!*'	'*Coquatrice!*'	'Saltflitch!'
'Tumbler!'	'Nightbird!'	'Fluter!'	'*Sourdite!*'
'*Poupinette!*'	'*Paillasse!*'	'*Coignée!*'	'Canvasback!'
'Mattressback!	'Rawhide!'	'Cockeye!'	'*Redresseuse!*'
'*Brimballeuse!*'	'*Capre!*'	'*Pelerine!*'	'Hipflipper!'
'Nannygoat!'	'Shortheels!'	'Crane!'	'*Personnière!*'
'*Chouette!*'	'*Paillarde!*'	'*Drôllesse!*'	'Hardtonguer!'
'Windowgirl!'	'Bumbessie!'	'Trotter!'	'*Ribaulde!*'
'*Wauve!*'	'*Image!*'	'*Pellice!*'	'Bedbug!'
'Lowgap!'	'Furrowbutt!'	'Fleecer!'	'*Posoera!*'
'*Peaultre!*'	'*Voyagère!*'	'*Toupie!*'	'Hamhocker!'
'Galleywench!'	'Pinkpot!'	'Fatback!'	'*Ricaldex!*'
'*Baque!*'	'*Femme de vie!*'	'*Saffrette!*'	'Bullseye!'
'Drab!'	'Rum-and-rut!'	'Nightbag!'	'*Sac-de-nuit!*'
'*Villotière!*'	'*Fellatrice!*' [...]	'*Reveleuse!*'	'Breechdropper!'

'Roussecaigne!'
'Giftbox!'
'Scaldrine!'
'Craterbutt!'
'Tendrière de
bouche et reins!'
'Pisspallet!'
'Presentière!'
'Narycherry!'
'Femme de mal
recapte!'
'Poxbox!'
'Touse!'
'Flapgap!'
'Rafatière!'
'Codhopper!'
'Courieuse!'
'Bellylass!'
'Gondinette!'
'Trollop!'
'Esquoceresse!'
'Peddlesnatch!'
'Folieuse!'
'Backgammon!'
'Gondine!'
'Joygirl!'
'Drue!'
'Prickpocket!'
'Galloise!' [...]
'Why, she's
naught but
a common
meatcooker!'
'And you a
janneton!' the
other replied
gleefully.

'Arsievarsie!'
'Fillette de pis!'
'Backscratcher!'
'Demoiselle
de morais!'
'Bumpbacon!'
'Gaultière!'
'Full-o'-tricks!'
'Ensaignante!'
'Pesthole!'
'Gast!'
'Romp!'
'Court talon!'
'Pigpoke!'
'Folle de corps!'
'Scabber!'
'Gouine!'
'Strumpet!'
'Fille de joie!'
'Gullybum!'
'Drouine!'
'Tess Tuppence!'
'Gaupe!'
'Slattern!'
'Entaille
d'amour!'
'Doxy!'
'Accrocheuse!'
'Chippie!'
'Cloistrière!'
'Puddletrotter!'
'Bagasser!'
'Hetaera!'
'Caignardière!'
'Pipecleaner!'
'Barathre!'
'Rumper!'

'Cambrouse!'
'Hotpot!'
'Alicaire!'
'Backbender!'
'Champisse!'
'Sink-o'-
perdition!'
'Cantonnière!'
'Leasepiece!'
'Ambubaye!'
'Spreadeagle!'
'Bassara!'
'Gutterflopper!'
'Bezoche!'
'Cockatrice!'
'Caille!'
'Sausage-grinder!'
'Bourbeteuse!'
'Cornergirl!'
'Braydone!'
'Codwinker!'
'Bonsoir!'
'Charlotte
Harlot!'
'Blanchisseuse
des pipes!'
'Nutcracker!'
'Balances de
boucher!'
'Meat-vendor!'
'Femme de péché!'
'Hedgewhore!'
'Lecheresse!'
'Ventrenter!'
'Hollière!'
'Lightheels!'
'Pantonière!'

'Gadder!'
'Grue!'
'Ragbag!'
'Musequine!'
'Fleshpot!'
'Louve!'
'Lecheress!'
'Martingale!'
'Tollhole!'
'Harrebane!'
'Pillowgut!'
'Marane!'
'Chamberpot!'
'Levrière
d'amour!'
'Swilltrough!'
'Pannanesse!'
'Potlicker!'
'Linatte coiffée!'
'Bedpan!'
'Hourieuse!'
'Cotwarmer!'
'Moché!'
'Stumpthumper!'
'Maxima!'
'Messalina!'
'Loudière!'
'Slopjar!'
'Manafle!'
'Hussy!'
'Lesbine!'
'Priest-layer!'
'Hore!'
'Harpy!'
'Mandrauna!'
'Diddler!'
'Maraude!'

'Foul-mouthed harridans!' Ebenezer cried, and fled through the first door he encountered.

The FILID

In ancient Ireland, there were strict grades among professional poets, which related to the number of stories each *fili* had memorized.

Ollam	350 stories	Macfuirmid	40 stories
Ánruth	175 stories	Fochloc	30 stories
Clí	87 stories	Taman	20 stories
Cano	60 stories	Drisiuc	10 stories
Dos	50 stories	Oblaire	5 stories

According to the eighth-century manuscript *Uraicecht na Ríar*, it took twelve years to reach the highest grade of *ollam*, at which point a *fili* was entitled to wear a cloak of crimson bird feathers and carry a wand of office.

VISIONS *of* FUTURES PAST

These novels were all set in the future, in a year that is now in the past.

		Published	Set
News from Nowhere	William Morris	1890	1952
The Black Cloud	Fred Hoyle	1957	1964
Slaughterhouse-Five	Kurt Vonnegut	1969	1976
The Napoleon of Notting Hill	G. K. Chesterton	1904	1984
Nineteen Eighty-Four	George Orwell	1949	1984
Do Androids Dream of Electric Sheep?	Philip K. Dick	1968	1992*
Memoirs of the Twentieth Century	Samuel Madden	1733	1997
Make Room! Make Room!	Harry Harrison	1966	1999
Looking Backward	Edward Bellamy	1888	2000
2001: A Space Odyssey	Arthur C. Clarke	1968	2001
The Astronauts	Stanisław Lem	1951	2003
Infinite Jest	David Foster Wallace	1996	2009†

* *Do Androids Dream of Electric Sheep?* was the basis for the 1982 film *Blade Runner*, set in 2019.
† See p.58.

The THIRTEEN TREASURES of the ISLAND of BRITAIN

Several early Welsh manuscripts describe thirteen magical treasures, or 'hallows', once belonging to the gods and heroes of Britain.* The wizard Merlin asked for these treasures, and their owners agreed to donate them if he could first get hold of the horn of the warrior Bran, a seemingly impossible task. Merlin persuaded Bran, however, and he collected the rest of the hallows and took them to a mysterious glass tower on Bardsey Island, off the Lleyn Peninsula in North Wales, where they remain in his keeping for the time of Britain's greatest need. Some say his tower is located above Elgar the Hermit's cave, on the western slope of the island.

The Mantle of Arthur	*makes the wearer invisible*
The Sword of Rhydderch the Generous	*bursts into flames if drawn by anyone else*
The Hamper of Gwyddno Longshank	*multiplies food a hundredfold*
The Horn of Bran the Miser	*contains any drink you wish for*
The Car of Morgan the Wealthy	*instantly transports you anywhere*
The Knife of Llawfrodedd the Bearded	*serves twenty-four men simultaneously*
The Cauldron of Dyrnwch the Giant	*boils for brave men, not for cowards*
The Whetstone of Tudwal Tudclyd	*sharpens the weapons of brave men, blunts those of cowards*
The Robe of Padarn Beisrudd	*suits noblemen, fits churls badly*
The Platter of Rhagennydd the Cleric	*serves any food you wish for*
The Chessboard of Gwenddoleu†	*a golden board with silver and crystal pieces, which play themselves*
The Mantle of Tegau of the Gold Breast	*covers faithful wives, stops at the knees of the unfaithful*
The Ring of Eluned the Blessed	*makes the wearer invisible when its stone is covered*

* Although various fifteenth- and sixteenth-century manuscripts agree on the number thirteen, the exact list of treasures is fluid. Some inventories include the Halter of Clydno Eidyn, which produces any horse one wishes for, and others the Coulter of Rhun the Giant, which makes any plough work magically until you ask it to stop.

† Though usually translated as 'chess', the game is actually *gwddybwyll*, an ancient Celtic board game whose name means 'wood sense'.

Some FORMS of POETRY

In contrast to free verse, fixed poetic forms have prescribed metres (see p.93) and rhyme schemes. In Europe, fixed forms originated in medieval France; in Asia, their roots lie in the *waka* poetry of ancient Japan. Their structure can allow poets a paradoxical liberty within constraints.

1 LINE	monoku • monostich
2 LINES	barzeletta • kural • landay • lục bát • masnavi • schuttelreim
3 LINES	haiku • kimo • sijo • soledad • stornello • terza rima • than-bauk • treochair • tripadi
4 LINES	clerihew* • dodoitsu • droigneach • endecha • imayo • kouta • kyrielle • pantoum • qijue • rinnard • rubaiyat • seadna • toddaid • trova
5 LINES	bob and wheel • elevenie • flamenca • limerick† • quintilla • tanka
6 LINES	clogyrnach • rime couée • sedoka • shadorma
7 LINES	rhyme royal • rondelet • seguidilla
8 LINES	chueh-chu • cyrch a chwta • huitain • ottava rima • rispetto • snam suad • strambotto • triolet
9 LINES	lai • Spenserian stanza • virelai
10 LINES	asefru • decima • dizain • espinela • Italian madrigal • Keatsian ode • ovillejo
11 LINES	curtal sonnet • roundel
12 LINES	rondine
13 LINES	English madrigal • rondel
14 LINES	bref double • sonnet
15 LINES	ya-du • rondeau
16 LINES	copla • quatern
19 LINES	villanelle
28 LINES	ballade
39 LINES	sestina‡
40 LINES	glosa
44 LINES	decima
60 LINES	chant royal

* A clerihew: four lines of verse With bad rhymes and metre that's worse. This humorous form, incidentally, Was invented by E. Clerihew Bentley. (See p.89.)

† See p.139.

‡ The sestina was invented in the twelfth century by the Provençal troubadour Arnaut Daniel. It consists of six stanzas of six lines and a three-line envoi. There are only six end-words, repeated in a different order in each stanza, with all six used in the envoi. 'The Complaint of Lisa' by Swinburne is a double sestina: it has twelve stanzas of twelve lines and a six-line envoi.

The TWELVE CAESARS

Suetonius was a private secretary to Emperor Hadrian in the second century AD and the author of a gossipy chronicle of Roman history, *The Twelve Caesars*, which supplies outrageous details about Julius Caesar and the first eleven emperors of Rome. Robert Graves, who translated *The Twelve Caesars* into English, called it 'the most fascinating and richest of all Latin histories'. He used it as the basis for his novel *I, Claudius*.

JULIUS CAESAR 'was something of a dandy'. ¶ AUGUSTUS had 'a constellation of seven birthmarks on his chest and stomach, exactly corresponding with the Great Bear'. ¶ TIBERIUS 'possessed the unusual power of seeing in the dark'. ¶ CALIGULA 'worked hard to make his naturally uncouth face even more repulsive'. ¶ CLAUDIUS 'planned an edict to legitimize the breaking of wind at table, either silently or noisily'. ¶ NERO 'never wore the same clothes twice'. ¶ GALBA 'was a heavy eater, in winter always breakfasting before daylight'. ¶ OTHO 'used a poultice of moist bread to retard the growth of his beard'. ¶ VITELLIUS 'would kill or torture anyone at all on the slightest pretext'. ¶ VESPASIAN 'often used obscene expressions'. ¶ TITUS 'owned a troop of inverts and eunuchs'. ¶ DOMITIAN 'would spend hours alone every day catching flies [...] and stabbing them with a needle-sharp pen'.

The SEVEN AGES *of* MAN

The melancholy Jaques, 'prince of philosophical idlers', as William Hazlitt called him, is an attendant on the banished Duke Senior in William Shakespeare's *As You Like It*, living in the Forest of Arden. 'All the world's a stage,' he muses, 'and all the men and women merely players.' He goes on to list the seven 'parts' that each man plays in his life:

Infant · School-boy · Lover · Soldier · Justice
Pantaloon · Second childishness*

* This final role is a sad list of negatives: 'Sans teeth, sans eyes, sans taste, sans everything.'

The LAWS *of* ROBOTICS

In *I, Robot*, the collection of short stories by Isaac Asimov, he listed the three fundamental laws of robotics, which he first devised in 1942.

1 — A robot may not injure a human being or, through inaction, allow a human being to come to harm.

2 — A robot must obey the orders given it by human beings except where such orders would conflict with the First Law.

3 — A robot must protect its own existence as long as such protection does not conflict with the First or Second Law.

Handbook of Robotics, 56th edition, 2058 A.D.

Some ANTICIPATORY PLAGIARISTS

Oulipo, or the *Ouvroir de littérature potentielle* ('Workshop of Potential Literature'), was founded in 1960 by Raymond Queneau and François Le Lionnais. This literary collective delights in constructing poems, stories and word games using constraints, rules and mathematical devices. Georges Perec and Italo Calvino were two of its best-known members. As well as inventing new rules, Oulipians take inspiration from earlier writers who used similar constraints: they call them 'anticipatory plagiarists'.

Jorge Luis Borges • Joe Brainard • Lewis Carroll • Arnaut Daniel
Robert Desnos • Alfred Jarry • George Herbert • Homer
Lasus of Hermione • Gottfried Leibniz • Ramón Llull • Lucretius
Herman Melville • Vladimir Nabokov • Edgar Allan Poe
François Rabelais • Raymond Roussel* • Christopher Smart
Su Hui† • Jonathan Swift • Stefan Themerson • Tryphidorus
Henry Vassall-Fox, Lord Holland • Yin Zhongkan

* Queneau praised the French poet Roussel for 'uniting the precision of the poet with the madness of the mathematician'.
† Lady Su Hui was a fourth-century Chinese poet, famous for constructing the *Xuanji Tu* ('Picture of the Turning Sphere' or 'Star Gauge'), an extremely complicated multiple palindrome that consists of a grid of 840 Chinese characters, from which you can read more than 3,000 rhyming poems.

The TEMPLE *of* BANNED BOOKS

In 2017, the Argentinian artist Marta Minujín constructed a vast replica of the Parthenon in Kassel, Germany, out of thousands of banned books. The following titles have been or are currently banned:

The Sorrows of Young Werther by Johann Wolfgang von Goethe	1775, in Leipzig, Germany, for sparking 'Werther Fever', a spate of suicides
The Rights of Man by Thomas Paine	1795–1822, in the UK, for sedition
Madame Bovary by Gustave Flaubert	1856–7, in France, for obscenity
Lysistrata by Aristophanes	1873–1930s, in the USA, for subversion
Ulysses by James Joyce	1922–36, in the UK, for obscenity
The Decameron by Giovanni Boccaccio	1927–36, in Australia, for obscenity
Lady Chatterley's Lover by D. H. Lawrence	1928–60, in the UK, for obscenity
Alice's Adventures in Wonderland by Lewis Carroll	1931, in Hunan, China, for portraying anthropomorphized animals
Brave New World by Aldous Huxley	1932–67, in Ireland, for obscenity
Tropic of Cancer by Henry Miller	1934–64, in the USA, for obscenity
Boy by James Hanley	1934–92, in the UK, for obscenity*
The Well of Loneliness by Radclyffe Hall	1938–73, in the UK, for lesbian content
A Short History of the World by H. G. Wells	1940–63, in Spain, for 'socialist inclinations'
Animal Farm by George Orwell	1945–90, in the USSR, for its anti-Soviet satire
The Second Sex by Simone de Beauvoir	1949–75, in Spain, for encouraging feminism
Frankenstein by Mary Shelley	1955, in South Africa, for indecency
Another Country by James Baldwin	1963–66, in Australia, for indecency
The Satanic Verses by Salman Rushdie	1989–today, in the Middle East, for blasphemy
American Psycho by Bret Easton Ellis	1995–2000, in Germany, for being 'harmful to minors'
The Da Vinci Code by Dan Brown	2004–today, in Lebanon, for blasphemy

* James Hanley's publishers were prosecuted after a Lancashire taxi driver and his wife took a copy of *Boy* to the police, having read only the blurb.

Some RIVER NOVELS

Romain Rolland, John Galsworthy and Roger Martin du Gard all won the Nobel Prize for their *romans-fleuves*, or 'river-novels'. Rolland inspired this term for a sequence of novels in his own *Jean-Christophe*. 'What is this work?' he asked. 'Jean-Christophe has always seemed to me to flow like a river.'

The Fortunes of War by Olivia Manning (Six volumes, 1960–80)
The Great Fortune · The Spoilt City · Friends and Heroes
The Danger Tree · The Battle Lost and Won · The Sum of Things

In Search of Lost Time by Marcel Proust (Seven volumes, 1913–27)
Swann's Way · In the Shadow of Young Girls in Flower · The Guermantes Way
Sodom and Gomorrah · The Prisoner · The Fugitive · Time Regained

The Thibaults by Roger Martin du Gard (Eight volumes, 1922–40)
The Grey Notebook · The Penitentiary · The Springtime of Life · The Consulting
Day · La Sorellina · The Death of the Father · Summer 1914 · Epilogue

The Forsyte Chronicles by John Galsworthy (Nine volumes, 1906–33)
The Man of Property · In Chancery · To Let · The White Monkey · The Silver
Spoon · Swan Song · Maid in Waiting · Flowering Wilderness · One More River

Jean-Christophe by Romain Rolland (Ten volumes, 1904–12)
Dawn · Morning · Youth · Revolt · The Marketplace · Antoinette
The House · Love and Friendship · The Burning Bush · The New Dawn

Strangers and Brothers by C. P. Snow (Eleven volumes, 1940–70)
Time of Hope · George Passant · The Conscience of the Rich
The Light and the Dark · The Masters · The New Men · Homecomings
The Affair · Corridors of Power · The Sleep of Reason · Last Things

A Dance to the Music of Time by Anthony Powell (Twelve volumes, 1951–75)
A Question of Upbringing · A Buyer's Market · The Acceptance World
At Lady Molly's · Casanova's Chinese Restaurant · The Kindly Ones
The Valley of Bones · The Soldier's Art · The Military Philosophers
Books Do Furnish a Room · Temporary Kings · Hearing Secret Harmonies

Pilgrimage by Dorothy Richardson (Thirteen volumes, 1915–67)
Pointed Roofs · Backwater · Honeycomb · The Tunnel · Interim · Deadlock
Revolving Lights · The Trap · Oberland · Dawn's Left Hand · Clear Horizon
Dimple Hill · March Moonlight

Some EQUELS

Philip Pullman coined the term 'equel' for works of parallel fiction that are neither prequels nor sequels but sit alongside an original text.

Marcel Proust *In Search of Lost Time*	*Albertine* Jacqueline Rose
Daniel Defoe *Robinson Crusoe*	*Foe* J. M. Coetzee
Beowulf	*Grendel* John Gardner
Virginia Woolf *Mrs Dalloway*	*The Hours* Michael Cunningham
Charles Dickens *Great Expectations*	*Jack Maggs* Peter Carey
Jane Austen *Pride and Prejudice*	*Longbourn* Jo Baker
Homer *The Odyssey*	*The Penelopiad* Margaret Atwood

FOWLER'S FORMS *of* HUMOUR

In 1926, the schoolmaster Henry Watson Fowler published *A Dictionary of Modern English Usage*, offering nuanced and witty advice on the correct use of the English language. Discussing the various forms of humour, Fowler included a 'tabular statement' to clear up 'some popular misconceptions'.

	MOTIVE	PROVINCE	METHOD	AUDIENCE
Humour	discovery	human nature	observation	the sympathetic
Wit	throwing light	words and ideas	surprise	the intelligent
Invective	discredit	misconduct	direct statement	the public
Satire	amendment	morals and manners	accentuation	the self-satisfied
Cynicism	self-justification	morals	exposure of nakedness	the respectable
Sarcasm	inflicting pain	faults and foibles	inversion	victim and bystander
Irony	exclusiveness	statement of facts	mystification	an inner circle
The Sardonic	self-relief	adversity	pessimism	self

The PROVERBS of HELL

In *The Marriage of Heaven and Hell*, William Blake imagined walking among the inspirational fires of Hell, 'delighted with the enjoyments of Genius'. He discourses with angels and devils and collects various local proverbs to illustrate 'the nature of infernal wisdom'. Here is a small selection:

Drive your cart and your plow over the bones of the dead.

The road of excess leads to the palace of wisdom.

The cut worm forgives the plow.

Dip him in the river who loves water.

A fool sees not the same tree that a wise man sees.

He whose face gives no light, shall never become a star.

No bird soars too high, if he soars with his own wings.

If the fool would persist in his folly he would become wise.

Excess of sorrow laughs. Excess of joy weeps.

The fox condemns the trap, not himself.

The bird a nest, the spider a web, man friendship.

What is now proved was once only imagin'd.

The cistern contains: the fountain overflows.

One thought fills immensity.

Think in the morning. Act in the noon. Eat in the evening.
  Sleep in the night.

The tygers of wrath are wiser than the horses of instruction.

You never know what is enough unless you know what is
  more than enough.

Listen to the fool's reproach! It is a kingly title!

The apple tree never asks the beech how he shall grow; nor the lion,
  the horse, how he shall take his prey.

When thou seest an Eagle, thou seest a portion of Genius; lift up thy head!

To create a little flower is the labour of ages.

The crow wish'd every thing was black; the owl that every thing was white.

Exuberance is Beauty.

*Improvement makes strait roads; but the crooked roads without Improvement
  are roads of Genius.*

Sooner murder an infant in its cradle than nurse unacted desires.

Truth can never be told so as to be understood, and not to be believ'd.

Enough! or Too much.

SEVEN SEVENS

This book contains seven lists of seven, not counting this one:

The Seven Ages of Man, see p.43
The Seven Basic Plots, see p.35
The Seven Commandments of Animalism, see p.31
The Seven Deadly Sins, see p.25
The Seven Dwarfs, see p.23
The Seven Types of Ambiguity, see p.136
The Seven Vowels, see p.126

A RIDE *around* ROUEN

Emma Bovary's second extra-marital affair, in *Madame Bovary* by Gustave Flaubert, begins with a lengthy love-making session inside a closed carriage around the streets of Rouen.* The increasingly fatigued cab-driver is forced to drive at random from before midday until six o'clock, visiting the various locations below, sometimes trotting gently, sometimes galloping. Vladimir Nabokov found this passage 'remarkably amusing'.

Rouen Cathedral → the rue Grand-Pont → the place des Arts → the quai Napoleon → the Pont Neuf → the statue of Pierre Corneille → the place La Fayette → the train station → the Seine towpath → Quatremares → Sotteville → La Grande-Chaussée → the rue d'Elbeuf → the Jardin des Plantes → Saint-Sever → the quai des Curandiers → the quai aux Meules → the Pont Neuf again → the place du Champ-de-Mars → the boulevard Bouvreuil → the boulevard Cauchoise → Mont-Riboudet → the hill of Deville → Saint-Pol → Lescure → Mont Gargan → La Rouge-Mare → the place du Gaillard-bois → the rue Maladrerie → the rue Dinanderie → Saint-Romain → Saint-Vivien → Saint-Maclou → Saint-Niçaise → the Customs House → the Vieille-Tour → the Trois Pipes → the cemetery → a back street of the Beauvoisine Quarter

---

* When the novel was first published serially, the editors of the magazine *Revue de Paris* suppressed this whole episode, informing readers of the omission in a footnote.

The BOOKS of ECCLESIASTES

'Of all I have ever seen or learned,' wrote Thomas Wolfe, 'that book seems to me the noblest, the wisest, and the most powerful expression of man's life upon this earth – and also the highest flower of poetry, eloquence, and truth.' Wolfe was describing the short biblical book of Ecclesiastes (or The Preacher), which collects the gnomic sayings of the son of King David of Jerusalem. The following novels take their titles from its verses.

Earth Abides George R. Stewart	One generation passeth away, and another generation cometh: but the earth abideth for ever. (1:4)
The Sun Also Rises Ernest Hemingway	The sun also ariseth, and the sun goeth down, and hasteth to his place where he arose. (1:5)
A Time to Kill John Grisham	A time to kill, and a time to heal; a time to break down, and a time to build up. (3:3)
A Time to Dance Melvyn Bragg (see p.10)	A time to weep, and a time to laugh; a time to mourn, and a time to dance. (3:4)
A Time to Keep Silence Patrick Leigh Fermor	A time to rend, and a time to sew; a time to keep silence, and a time to speak. (3:7)
A Time to Love *and a Time to Die* Erich Maria Remarque	A time to love, and a time to hate; a time of war, and a time of peace. (3:8)
And a Threefold Cord Alex La Guma	And if one prevail against him, two shall withstand him; and a threefold cord is not quickly broken. (4:12)
Evil Under the Sun Agatha Christie	There is an evil which I have seen under the sun, and it is common among men. (6:1)
The House of Mirth Edith Wharton	The heart of the wise is in the house of mourning; but the heart of fools is in the house of mirth. (7:4)
The Golden Bowl Henry James	Or ever the silver cord be loosed, or the golden bowl be broken. (12:6)

The HOUR of the STAR

The last novel by the Brazilian author Clarice Lispector, *A hora da estrela*, tells the story of Macabéa, who moves from rural Alagoas, where Lispector lived as a child, to Rio de Janeiro. 'It's an unfinished book because it's still waiting for an answer,' she wrote. 'An answer I hope someone in the world can give me. You?' She included a list of alternative titles on the title page.

It's All My Fault · *The Hour of the Star* · *Let Her Deal With It*
The Right to Scream · *As For the Future* · *Singing the Blues* · *She Doesn't Know How to Scream* · *A Sense of Loss* · *Whistling in the Dark Wind*
I Can't Do Anything · *Account of the Preceding Facts* · *Cheap Tearjerker*
Discreet Exit Through the Back Door

Some LITERARY PATRONS

Ever since Maecenas supported Virgil, impecunious writers have relied on wealthy sponsors to pay their living expenses and they have dedicated works to them in return. In a literary world dominated historically by men, patronage has also been a vicarious way for women of means to express creativity. These writers, for example, all had female patrons:

William Blake	Harriet Mathew
Robert Burns	Jane Gordon, Duchess of Gordon
John Gay	Catherine Douglas, Duchess of Queensberry
Kahlil Gibran	Mary Haskell
Aldous Huxley	Lady Ottoline Morrell
Ben Jonson	Lucy Russell, Countess of Bedford
James Joyce	Harriet Shaw Weaver
François Rabelais	Queen Marguerite de Navarre
Edmund Spenser	Mary Sidney, Countess of Pembroke
Montesquieu	Claudine-Alexandrine Guérin de Tencin
Rainer Maria Rilke	Princess Marie von Thurn und Taxis
W. B. Yeats	Isabella Augusta, Lady Gregory

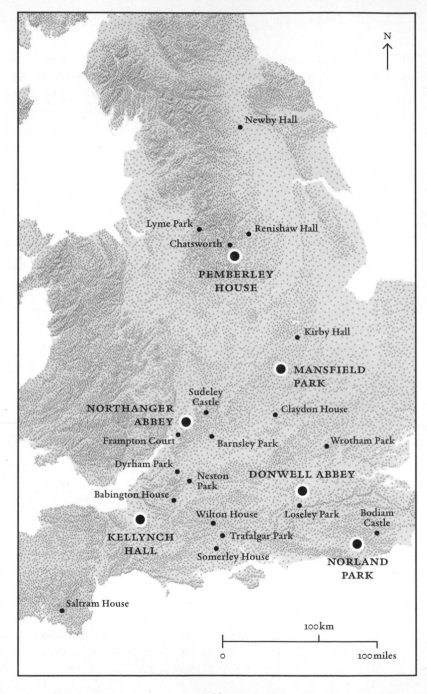

N

Newby Hall

Lyme Park
Renishaw Hall
Chatsworth
**PEMBERLEY
HOUSE**

Kirby Hall

**MANSFIELD
PARK**

Sudeley
Castle
**NORTHANGER
ABBEY**
Claydon House
Frampton Court
Barnsley Park
Wrotham Park

Dyrham Park
Neston
Park
DONWELL ABBEY
Babington House
Wilton House
Loseley Park
Bodiam
Castle
**KELLYNCH
HALL**
Trafalgar Park
Somerley House
**NORLAND
PARK**

Saltram House

100km

0   100miles

The GREAT HOUSES *of* JANE AUSTEN

In each of Jane Austen's novels there is a 'Great House', often home to an eligible man in possession of a good fortune, who generally invites the book's heroine to be his wife. These houses have been portrayed by various stately homes in different television and film adaptations over the years, the locations of which are shown on the map opposite.

Northanger Abbey, Gloucestershire
in *Northanger Abbey*
'a large court [...] rich in
Gothic ornaments'

1987 Bodiam Castle, East Sussex
2007 Lismore Castle, County
    Waterford

Norland Park, Sussex
in *Sense and Sensibility*
'their estate was large [...]
a prodigious beautiful place'

1981 Babington House, Somerset
1995 Saltram House, Devon
2008 Wrotham Park, Hertfordshire

Pemberley House, Derbyshire
in *Pride and Prejudice*
'a large, handsome stone
building, standing well on
rising ground'

1967 Dyrham Park, Gloucestershire
1980 Renishaw Hall, Derbyshire
1995 Lyme Park, Derbyshire
2005 Chatsworth, Derbyshire

Mansfield Park, Northamptonshire
in *Mansfield Park*
'a real park, five miles round,
a spacious modern-built house'

1983 Somerley House, Hampshire
1999 Kirby Hall, Northamptonshire
2007 Newby Hall, North Yorkshire

Donwell Abbey, Surrey
in *Emma*
'covering a good deal of ground,
rambling and irregular, with
many comfortable, and one or
two handsome rooms'

1996 Claydon House,
    Buckinghamshire
1996 Sudeley Castle, Gloucestershire
2009 Loseley Park, Surrey
2020 Wilton House, Wiltshire

Kellynch Hall, Somerset
in *Persuasion*
'a character of hospitality and
ancient dignity'

1971 Frampton Court,
    Gloucestershire
1995 Barnsley Park, Gloucestershire
2007 Neston Park, Wiltshire
2022 Trafalgar Park, Wiltshire

The SIZE *of* BOOKS

When printing a book, several pages are printed at once on to large sheets of paper. These are then folded and cut to make 'signatures', which are bound together. Traditionally, the size of a book was a combination of the original paper size and the number of times it had been folded.

TRADITIONAL PAPER SIZES

Atlas	34 × 26 inches	Demy	22½ × 17½ inches
Imperial	30 × 22 inches	Crown	20 × 15 inches
Elephant	28 × 23 inches	Foolscap*	16 × 13 inches
Royal	25 × 20 inches		

TRADITIONAL FOLDING PATTERNS

Folio	in half once, to make two leaves (4 pages)
Quarto	in half twice, to make four leaves (8 pages)
Octavo	in half three times, to make eight leaves (16 pages)
Duodecimo	in three, then in half twice, to make twelve leaves (24 pages)
Sextodecimo	in half four times, to make sixteen leaves (32 pages)

SOME FINISHED BOOK SIZES

Royal Folio	20 × 12½ inches	(508 × 318 mm)
Demy Quarto	11¼ × 8¾ inches	(286 × 222 mm)
Imperial Octavo	11 × 7½ inches	(279 × 191 mm)
Crown Quarto	10 × 7½ inches	(254 × 191 mm)
Demy Octavo	8⅜ × 5⅝ inches	(213 × 143 mm)
Crown Octavo	7½ × 5 inches	(191 × 127 mm)
Foolscap Octavo	6½ × 4 inches	(165 × 102 mm)

Today printers use standardized book sizes, although some of the traditional names have been preserved.

Crown Quarto	246 × 189 mm	B-format†	198 × 129 mm
Royal	234 × 156 mm	A-format	178 × 110 mm
Demy	216 × 138 mm		

---

* Foolscap paper is named after the watermark of a fool's cap and bells which was associated with this size of paper in the fifteenth century.

† The book you are holding is printed in B-format.

TOLSTOY'S BATTLES

Leo Tolstoy's *War and Peace* presents a tapestry of characters and events during the Napoleonic Wars, with moments of peace broken by periods of bloody war. The principal campaigns it depicts are those of the War of the Third Coalition, which culminates in Napoleon's decisive victory at Austerlitz in 1805; and Napoleon's invasion of Russia, which ended in disaster for the French in 1812. The following battles feature in the novel:

1805
The Battle of Schöngrabern · The Battle of Austerlitz

1812
The Battle of Ostrovno · The Battle of Borodino · The Battle of Tarutino · The Battle of Maloyaroslavets · The Battle of Vyazma
The Battle of Krasnoye · The Battle of the Berezina

To PACK *and* WEAR

When Joan Didion was working as a reporter in Hollywood in the 1960s, she kept a list taped inside her closet door, which allowed her to pack without thinking and leave for assignments at short notice. She reprinted the list in her essay 'The White Album'. 'There is on this list one significant omission,' she wrote, 'one article I needed and never had: a watch.'

To Pack and Wear:
    2 skirts · 2 jerseys or leotards · 1 pullover sweater · 2 pair shoes
    stockings* · bra · nightgown, robe, slippers · cigarettes · bourbon
    bag with shampoo · toothbrush and paste · Basis soap · razor,
        deodorant · aspirin, prescriptions, Tampax · face cream,
        powder, baby oil

To Carry:
    mohair throw · typewriter · 2 legal pads and pens · files · house key

---

* 'Notice the deliberate anonymity of costume,' she wrote: 'in a skirt, a leotard, *and stockings*, I could pass on either side of the culture.'

Some AUCTORIAL ADJECTIVES

Aristotelian • (*Samuel*) Beckettian • (*Jeremy*) Benthamite
(*Jorge Luis*) Borgesian • (*Bertolt*) Brechtian • (*Lord*) Byronic
(*René Des*)cartesian • (*Geoffrey*) Chaucerian • (*Anton*) Chekhovian
(*Charles*) Darwinian • (*Charles*) Dickensian • (*Sigmund*) Freudian
(*Thomas*) Hobbesian • Homeric • Horatian • (*Henry*) Jamesian
(*Samuel*) Johnsonian • (*James*) Joycean • Juvenalian • (*Franz*) Kafkaesque
(*John*) Keatsian • (*Niccolò*) Machiavellian • (*Thomas*) Malthusian
(*Christopher*) Marlovian • (*Leopold von Sacher-*)Masochist
(*Friedrich*) Nietzschean • (*George*) Orwellian • (*Samuel*) Pepysian
(*Harold*) Pinteresque • Platonic • (*Marcel*) Proustian • (*François*) Rabelaisian
(*Marquis de*) Sadist • (*William*) Shakespearean • (*George Bernard*) Shavian
(*Edmund*) Spenserian • Virgilian • (*Oscar*) Wildean

KAFKA'S LAST REQUEST

When Franz Kafka died in 1924, only a fraction of his writing had been published. His friend Max Brod found a huge archive of manuscript drafts, including the novels *The Trial* and *The Castle* and the stories 'The Burrow', 'The Village Schoolmaster' and 'The Great Wall of China'. Brod also found two notes addressed to him. 'Dearest Max,' read one. 'My last request: Everything I leave behind me [...] is to be burned unread and to the last page.' The other repeated this request but made exception for six already published works.* Luckily for us, Brod did not burn the manuscripts; if he had, we might have known only the following works by Kafka.

A Country Doctor† • 'A Hunger Artist' • 'In the Penal Colony'
'The Judgement' • 'The Metamorphosis' • 'The Stoker'‡

---

* 'I do not mean that I wish them to be reprinted and handed down to posterity,' Kafka clarified. 'On the contrary, should they disappear altogether that would please me best. Only, since they do exist, I do not wish to hinder anyone who may want to, from keeping them.'

† Kafka's second collection of stories includes 'Before the Law', which was written as part of his posthumously published novel, *The Trial*.

‡ 'The Stoker' was first published as a standalone pamphlet, but it was written as the opening chapter of Kafka's first novel, *Amerika*.

The ROUGON-MACQUART CYCLE

Émile Zola published a cycle of twenty novels between 1871 and 1893, to which he gave the collective title *Les Rougon-Macquart*. The novels present a 'natural and social history' of two branches of a fictional family, living during the French Second Empire (1852–70). In his preface to *Doctor Pascal*, the final instalment, Zola recommended reading the novels in the following order, so as to cover the Rougons first and then the Macquarts:

1. *The Fortune of the Rougons* (1871)
2. *His Excellency Eugène Rougon* (1876)
3. *The Kill* (1871–2)
4. *Money* (1891)
5. *The Dream* (1888)
6. *The Conquest of Plassans* (1874)
7. *Pot Luck* (1882)
8. *The Ladies' Delight* (1883)
9. *The Sin of Abbé Mouret* (1875)
10. *A Love Story* (1878)
11. *The Belly of Paris* (1873)
12. *The Bright Side of Life* (1884)
13. *The Drinking Den* (1877)
14. *The Masterpiece* (1886)
15. *The Beast Within* (1890)
16. *Germinal* (1885)
17. *Nana* (1880)
18. *The Earth* (1887)
19. *The Debacle* (1892)
20. *Doctor Pascal* (1893)

Zola planned the whole Rougon-Macquart cycle before he began writing. In 1878 he drew up the family tree below and modified it several times.

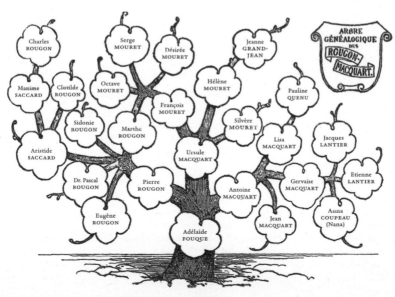

The YEARS of SUBSIDIZED TIME

David Foster Wallace's *Infinite Jest* (1996) is set in a future where global corporations sponsor (and name) each calendar year. Most of the novel takes place during the Year of the Depend Adult Undergarment, which, according to the critic Stephen J. Burn, corresponds to 2009.

The Year of the Whopper · The Year of the Tucks Medicated Pad · The Year of the Trial-Size Dove Bar · The Year of the Perdue Wonderchicken · The Year of the Whisper-Quiet Maytag Dishmaster · The Year of the Yushityu 2007 Mimetic-Resolution-Cartridge-View-Motherboard-Easy-To-Install-Upgrade For Infernatron/InterLace TP Systems For Home, Office Or Mobile · The Year of Dairy Products from the American Heartland · The Year of the Depend Adult Undergarment · The Year of Glad

SUCH STUFF *as* DREAMS *are* MADE ON

Shakespeare is the most filmed author in any language, with more than 400 movie adaptations of his works, including the following:

Yellow Sky (1948)	*The Tempest*
Throne of Blood (1957)	*Macbeth*
An Honourable Murder (1960)	*Julius Caesar*
West Side Story (1961)	*Romeo and Juliet*
Carry on Cleo (1964)	*Antony and Cleopatra*
Ran (1985)	*King Lear*
Big Business (1988)	*The Comedy of Errors*
My Own Private Idaho (1991)	*Henry IV, Parts 1 & 2, and Henry V*
The Lion King (1994)	*Hamlet*
10 Things I Hate About You (1999)	*The Taming of the Shrew*
Get Over It (2001)	*A Midsummer Night's Dream*
O (2001)	*Othello*
She's the Man (2006)	*Twelfth Night*

The BOTTOM-WIPERS

In *Gargantua*, François Rabelais's prequel to *Pantagruel*, the giant Gargantua conducts some original research. 'I have,' he says, 'found out a means to wipe my bum, the most lordly, the most excellent, and the most convenient that ever was seen.' He investigates the following 'bumfodders':

Once I did wipe me
    with a gentle-woman's velvet mask,
    with one of their hoods,
    with a lady's neckerchief,
    with some ear-pieces of hers made of crimson satin,
    with a page's cap, garnished with a feather after the Switzers' fashion,
    with a March-cat,
    with my mother's gloves,
    with sage, with fennel, with anet, with marjoram, with roses, with
        gourd-leaves, with beets, with colewort, with leaves of the vine-tree,
        with mallows, wool-blade, which is a tail-scarlet, with lettuce, and
        with spinach leaves,
    with mercury, with parsley, with nettles, with comfrey, with my braguette,
    in the sheets, in the coverlet, in the curtains, with a cushion, with arras
        hangings, with a green carpet, with a table-cloth, with a napkin, with
        a handkerchief, with a combing-cloth,
    with hay, with straw, with thatch-rushes, with flax, with wool, with paper,
    with a kerchief, with a pillow, with a pantoufle, with a pouch, with
        a pannier, with a hat,
    with a hen, with a cock, with a pullet, with a calf's skin, with a hare, with
        a pigeon, with a cormorant, with an attorney's bag, with a montero,
        with a coif, with a falconer's lure.

But, to conclude, I say and maintain, that of all torcheculs, arsewisps, bumfodders, tail-napkins, bunghole cleansers, and wipe-breeches, there is none in the world comparable to the neck of a goose, that is well downed, if you hold her head betwixt your legs. And believe me therein upon mine honour, for you will thereby feel in your nockhole a most wonderful pleasure, both in regard of the softness of the said down and of the temporate heat of the goose, which is easily communicated to the bum-gut and the rest of the inwards, in so far as to come even to the regions of the heart and brains.

Some FICTIONAL WORKS *in* WORKS *of* FICTION

Writing books is 'a laborious madness and an impoverishing one', said Jorge Luis Borges, '[...] setting out in five hundred pages an idea that can be perfectly related orally in five minutes'. Borges liked to write very short stories about very large books, such as *The Encyclopaedia of Tlön* or *The Book of Sand*. Here are some other works that have never been written:

The Grasshopper Lies Heavy	in *The Man in the High Castle*
Hawthorne Abendsen	Philip K. Dick
Mad Trist	in 'The Fall of the House of Usher'
Sir Launcelot Canning	Edgar Allan Poe
Vulture Hill	in *Nazi Literature in the Americas**
Irma Carrasco	Roberto Bolaño
Gigamesh	in *A Perfect Vacuum*†
Patrick Hannahan	Stanisław Lem
The Prismatic Bezel	in *The Real Life of Sebastian Knight*
Sebastian Knight	Vladimir Nabokov
The Duke's Daughter	in *Little Women*
Jo March	Louisa May Alcott
Jacob Wrestling	in *I Capture the Castle*
James Mortmain	Dodie Smith
The Affair of the Second Goldfish	in *Cards on the Table*
Ariadne Oliver	Agatha Christie
The God in the Labyrinth	in 'A Survey of the Works of Herbert Quain'
Herbert Quain	Jorge Luis Borges
Golden Hours	in *The Third Policeman*
De Selby	Flann O'Brien
The Gutless Wonder	in *Slaughterhouse-Five*
Kilgore Trout	Kurt Vonnegut

---

* *Nazi Literature in the Americas* is an exhaustive compendium of fictional fascist authors and their works. The *Financial Times* called it 'the best and weirdest kind of literary game'.

† *A Perfect Vacuum* contains fifteen reviews of imaginary books and a review of *A Perfect Vacuum* itself. The books reviewed include *Sexplosion* by Simon Merrill, *Gruppenführer Louis XVI* by Alfred Zellerman and *Being Inc.* by Alastair Waynewright.

The CLUB

Founded in 1764 by the artist Joshua Reynolds in order to provide Dr Samuel Johnson with stimulating conversation, the Club was a social and literary discussion group, which met at the Turk's Head pub on Gerrard Street in Soho, London. There were nine original members; later members included James Boswell, David Garrick, Edward Gibbon and Adam Smith.

Topham Beauclerk · Edmund Burke · Anthony Chamier
Oliver Goldsmith · John Hawkins · Samuel Johnson
Bennet Langton · Christopher Nugent · Joshua Reynolds

The DULUOZ LEGEND

'My work comprises one vast book like Proust's *Remembrances of Things Past*,' wrote Jack Kerouac in 1960, 'except that my remembrances are written on the run instead of afterwards in a sick bed.' Most of Kerouac's novels are autobiographical and he saw them as chapters in a self-portrait which he called *The Duluoz Legend*. Kerouac died in 1969, leaving his project incomplete, but you can still trace his life story through these twelve titles:

	YEARS COVERED	YEARS WRITTEN
Visions of Gerard	1922–6	1956
Doctor Sax	1930–36	1952
Maggie Cassidy	1938–9	1953
Vanity of Duluoz	1935–46	1967
On the Road (see p.74)	1946–50	1948–56
Visions of Cody	1946–52	1951–52
The Subterraneans	1953	1953
Tristessa	1955–6	1955–6
The Dharma Bums	1955–6	1957
Desolation Angels	1956–61	1956–61
Big Sur	1960	1961
Satori in Paris	1965	1965–6

J'AIME, JE N'AIME PAS

In *Roland Barthes* by Roland Barthes, the French literary theorist presented a fragmented and idiosyncratic self-portrait, composed of vignettes, photographs, epiphanies and lists, including the following inventory of likes and dislikes, which, he said, comprised his distinctive 'bodily enigma'.

J'aime, je n'aime pas – I like, I don't like

I like: salad, cinnamon, cheese, pimento, marzipan, the smell of new-cut hay (why doesn't someone with a 'nose' make such a perfume), roses, peonies, lavender, champagne, loosely held political convictions, Glenn Gould, too-cold beer, flat pillows, toast, Havana cigars, Handel, slow walks, pears, white peaches, cherries, colours, watches, all kinds of writing pens, desserts, unrefined salt, realistic novels, the piano, coffee, Pollock, Twombly, all romantic music, Sartre, Brecht, Verne, Fourier, Eisenstein, trains, Médoc wine, having change, *Bouvard and Pécuchet*,* walking in sandals on the lanes of southwest France, the bend of the Adour seen from Doctor L.'s house, the Marx Brothers, the mountains at seven in the morning leaving Salamanca, etc.

I don't like: white Pomeranians, women in slacks, geraniums, strawberries, the harpsichord, Miró, tautologies, animated cartoons, Arthur Rubinstein, villas, the afternoon, Satie, Bartók, Vivaldi, telephoning, children's choruses, Chopin's concertos, Burgundian branles and Renaissance dances, the organ, Marc-Antoine Charpentier, his trumpets and kettledrums, the politico-sexual, scenes, initiatives, fidelity, spontaneity, evenings with people I don't know, etc.

I like, I don't like: this is of no importance to anyone; this, apparently, has no meaning. And yet all this means: *my body is not the same as yours*. Hence, in this anarchic foam of tastes and distastes, a kind of listless blur, gradually appears the figure of a bodily enigma, requiring complicity or irritation.

* *Bouvard and Pécuchet* was the unfinished, encyclopaedic novel on which Gustave Flaubert was working when he died. It was also a favourite of Jorge Luis Borges, who observed that Flaubert, having invented the realist novel, 'was also the first to shatter it' (see p.49 and p.28).

The THREE MUSKETEERS

Athos · Porthos · Aramis

BANKNOTES *of the* POUND STERLING

The first person to appear on a Bank of England banknote was Queen Elizabeth II in 1960. Ten years later, the new £20 note featured William Shakespeare. Since then, the following authors have been depicted:

BANK OF ENGLAND

Winston Churchill	£5	2016–present
Charles Dickens	£10	1992–2003
Charles Darwin	£10	2000–2018
Jane Austen	£10	2017–present
William Shakespeare	£20	1970–1993
Adam Smith	£20	2007–2022

BANK OF SCOTLAND

Sir Walter Scott*	all	1995–present

ROYAL BANK OF SCOTLAND

Nan Shepherd	£5	2016–present
Mary Somerville	£10	2016–present

CLYDESDALE BANK

Robert Burns	£5	1997–2009
Robert Burns	£10	2009–present
Adam Smith	£50	1997–2009

* Since 1921, the Bank of England has had a monopoly on issuing paper currency in England and Wales, but in Scotland and Northern Ireland seven banks retain the right to issue notes, largely thanks to a campaign waged by the novelist Sir Walter Scott, under the pseudonym Malachi Malagrowther. As a token of thanks, all Bank of Scotland notes display Scott's portrait.

NO THANKS

In 1935, e e cummings self-published a collection of poetry with the help of his mother. He had intended to call the book *70 Poems*, but after fourteen publishing houses turned it down, he changed the title to *No Thanks* and dedicated it to them. He ordered the list to look like funerary urn.

TO

Farrar & Rinehart

Simon & Schuster

Coward-McCann

Limited Editions

Harcourt, Brace

Random House

Equinox Press

Smith & Haas

Viking Press

Knopf

Dutton

Harper's

Scribner's

Covici-Friede

AUSTIN'S ROSE CULTIVARS

The English rosarian David Austin had a fifty-year career breeding roses, and gave many of his cultivars names with literary associations. This small selection demonstrates the breadth of his reading:

The Wife of Bath (1969) • Robbie Burns (1985) • Prospero (1992)
Jude the Obscure (1995) • A Shropshire Lad (1996) • Christopher
Marlowe (2002) • Young Lycidas (2008)* • Lady of Shalott (2009)
Sir Walter Scott (2015) • Roald Dahl (2016) • The Ancient
Mariner (2015) • Emily Brontë (2018) • The Mill on the Floss (2018)

---

* Incidentally, John Milton introduced the word 'fragrance' to the English language, in *Paradise Lost*.

Some SCHOOLS of LITERATURE

'Thank God, I never was sent to School,' wrote William Blake, 'To be Flogg'd into following the Stile of a Fool.' Some schools in literature are pleasant and jolly, but most are dull, cruel and, in some cases, deadly.

Brookfield School	*Goodbye, Mr Chips*	James Hilton
Miss Cackle's Academy	*The Worst Witch*	Jill Murphy
Carne School	*A Murder of Quality*	John le Carré
Crunchem Hall	*Matilda*	Roald Dahl
Dorset Academy	*A Good School*	Richard Yates
Dotheboys Hall	*Nicholas Nickleby*	Charles Dickens
Enfield Tennis Academy	*Infinite Jest*	David Foster Wallace
Hailsham	*Never Let Me Go*	Kazuo Ishiguro
Hampden College	*The Secret History*	Donna Tartt
Hogwarts School	The *Harry Potter* series	J. K. Rowling
Linbury Court	*Jennings Goes to School*	Anthony Buckeridge
Llanabba Castle	*Decline and Fall*	Evelyn Waugh
Lowood Institution	*Jane Eyre*	Charlotte Brontë
Malory Towers	The *Malory Towers* series	Enid Blyton
Marcia Blaine School	*The Prime of Miss Jean Brodie*	Muriel Spark
Meadowbank School	*Cat Among the Pigeons*	Agatha Christie
Pencey Preparatory	*The Catcher in the Rye*	J. D. Salinger
Piorkowksi's	*Ferdydurke*	Witold Gombrowicz
Les Ruches	*Olivia*	Olivia*
Saint-Agathe	*Le Grand Meaulnes*	Alain-Fournier
St Custard's	The *Molesworth* series†	Geoffrey Willans & Ronald Searle
St Trinian's	*The Terror of St Trinian's*	Ronald Searle
Sawston School	*The Longest Journey*	E. M. Forster
Wortle's Academy	*Dr Wortle's School*	Anthony Trollope

* 'Olivia' was the pseudonym of Dorothy Bussy, Lytton Strachey's sister, who based her only novel on her own schoolgirl infatuation with a female teacher at her French finishing school.
† Nigel Molesworth, 'the goriller of 3B', explains that schools are 'nothing but kanes, lat. french, geog. hist. algy, geom, headmasters, skool dogs, skool sossages, my bro molesworth 2 and MASTERS everywhere. The only good things about skool are the BOYS wizz who are noble brave fearless etc. although you hav various swots, bullies, cissies, milksops greedy guts and oiks with whom i am forced to mingle hem-hem. In fact any skool is a bit of a shambles.'

BOARD GAMES *in* BOOKS

Board games imitate the real world in microcosm and have often proved fruitful metaphors. In Chaucer's *The Book of the Duchess*, for example, a game of chess represents the vicissitudes of life; in Middleton's play *A Game at Chess*, set on a chessboard, the game serves as an anti-Spanish satire; and in Shakespeare's *The Tempest*, a game of chess reflects the growing affection between Miranda and Ferdinand. Here are some more literary games:

AZAD* →	*The Player of Games* by Iain M. Banks	**CHESS** →	*Murphy* by Samuel Beckett	*The Chessmen of Mars* by Edgar Rice Burroughs
Chess, or The Royal Game by Stefan Zweig	*The Queen's Gambit* by Walter Tevis	*Life A User's Manual* by Georges Perec (see p.99)	*The Luzhin Defense* by Vladimir Nabokov ←	↓ *Through the Looking-Glass* by Lewis Carroll
THE GLASS BEAD GAME*	*The Glass Bead Game* by Hermann Hesse	**GO** →	*The Master of Go* by Yasunari Kawabata	ℰ by Jacques Roubaud
Jumanji by Chris Van Allsburg ←	**JUMANJI***	*Interstellar Pig* by William Sleator ←	**INTER-STELLAR PIG***	↓ *The Girl Who Played Go* by Sa Shan
RISE AND DECLINE OF THE THIRD REICH →	*The Third Reich* by Roberto Bolaño	**THUD** →	*Going Postal* by Terry Pratchett	*Thud!* by Terry Pratchett

* These are all fictional games. Azad is played on large three-dimensional boards and determines the social hierarchy of the Empire of Azad in the Small Magellanic Cloud; The Glass Bead Game is an abstract synthesis of all human culture, played by monk-like intellectuals in the ivory-tower province of Castalia; Interstellar Pig is both a race to keep the smiling pink 'Piggy' card and a battle for cosmic survival; and Jumanji introduces sub-Saharan wildlife and undergrowth to a small town in America. Thud is a real board game, developed by Terry Pratchett and Trevor Truran in 2002, which features briefly in *Going Postal* (2004) and heavily in *Thud!* (2005).

The WANDRING WOOD

In *The Faerie Queene* by Edmund Spenser, the Redcrosse Knight is riding with his lady and her dwarf, when a sudden storm forces them to shelter in a wood, and they get lost among the many types of tree:

> The sayling PINE, the CEDAR proud and tall,
> The vine-prop ELME, the POPLAR never dry,
> The builder OAKE, sole king of forrests all,
> The ASPINE good for staves, the CYPRESSE funerall.
> The LAURELL, meed of mightie Conquerours,
> And Poets sage, the FIRRE that weepeth still,
> The WILLOW worne of forlorne Paramours,
> The EUGH obedient to the benders will,
> The BIRCH for shaftes, the SALLOW for the mill,
> The MIRRHE sweete bleeding in the bitter wound,
> The warlike BEECH, the ASH for nothing ill,
> The fruitfull OLIVE, and the PLATANE round,
> The carver HOLME, the MAPLE seldom inward sound.

The POLES

The north and south polar regions are two of the least hospitable areas of the planet; for that reason, perhaps, several books have been set there.

THE ARCTIC	THE ANTARCTIC
The Blazing World by Margaret Cavendish	*The Birthday Boys* by Beryl Bainbridge
The Frozen Deep by Wilkie Collins & Charles Dickens	*A Strange Manuscript Found in a Copper Cylinder* by James De Mille
The Call of the Wild by Jack London	*At the Mountains of Madness* by H. P. Lovecraft
Ice Station Zebra by Alistair MacLean	
Northern Lights by Philip Pullman	*The Narrative of Arthur Gordon Pym of Nantucket* by Edgar Allan Poe
Frankenstein by Mary Shelley	*An Antarctic Mystery* by Jules Verne
The Purple Cloud by M. P. Shiel	

The GHOST CLUB

Founded in 1862 in London, the Ghost Club is the world's oldest society for the investigation of supernatural phenomena. Members undertake practical investigations of unexplained occurrences and meet to discuss ghostly subjects. Over the years, members have included:

Algernon Blackwood · Charles Dickens · Arthur Conan Doyle
Julian Huxley · Arthur Koestler · Arthur Machen · Siegfried Sassoon
Osbert Sitwell · Dennis Wheatley · Colin Wilson · W. B. Yeats

MILLER'S COMMANDMENTS

In 1932, while the American author Henry Miller was living in Clichy, in northern Paris, working on what would become *Tropic of Cancer*, he compiled a list of 'commandments' to keep himself focused on his work.

1. Work on one thing at a time until finished.
2. Start no more new books, add no more new material to 'Black Spring'.
3. Don't be nervous. Work calmly, joyously, recklessly on whatever is in hand.
4. Work according to Program and not according to mood. Stop at the appointed time!*
5. When you can't *create* you can *work*.
6. Cement a little every day, rather than add new fertilizers.
7. Keep human! See people, go places, drink if you feel like it.
8. Don't be a draught-horse! Work with pleasure only.
9. Discard the Program when you feel like it – but go back to it next day. *Concentrate. Narrow down. Exclude.*
10. Forget the books you want to write. Think only of the book you *are* writing.
11. Write first and always. Painting, music, friends, cinema, all these come afterwards.

---

* Miller devised a 'daily program' for himself: in the mornings, 'if groggy, type notes [...] if in fine fettle, write'; in the afternoons, 'work on section in hand [...] no intrusions, no diversions'; in the evenings: 'See friends. Read in cafés. [...] Paint if empty or tired.'

Kama, 'pleasure', is one of the four goals of Hindu life, along with *dharma* ('righteousness'), *artha* ('prosperity') and *moksha* ('liberation'). The *Kama Sutra* by Vātsyāyana provides guidance on the pursuit of pleasure in all its forms, but it has always been most famous as a sex manual. 'It is said that sexual union has sixty-four elements,' Vātsyāyana explains. '[...] Sexual union has eight parts, and each of these has eight varieties.'

EMBRACING 'The touch' [...] 'the thrust' [...] 'the rub' [...] 'the hard embrace' [...] the 'twining creeper', the 'climbing a tree', the 'sesame seeds and rice grains' and the 'milk and water'.

KISSING There are three types of kisses for a virgin girl: the nominal, the throbbing and the brushing kiss. [...] There are four other kisses: from the front, from the side, from the back and the hard kiss. A fifth one consists of bunching the other's lips with one's fingers into a ball and kissing them hard without using the teeth. This is the pressing kiss.

SCRATCHING Eight kinds of marks are made with fingernails: the 'mixed', the 'half-moon', the 'circle', the 'line', the 'tiger's claw', the 'peacock's foot', the 'leaping hare' and the 'lotus leaf'.

BITING There are different kinds of bite: the 'hidden', the 'swollen', the 'spot', the 'garland of spots', the 'coral and gem', the 'garland of gems', the 'piece of cloud' and the 'boar's bite'.

COITION Where the male organ is larger in proportion to the female, there are three possibilities: the 'dilation', the 'yawn' and that named 'Indrani'. [...] Where the woman is larger than the man, there are four methods: the 'box', the 'squeeze', the 'encirclement' and 'like a mare'.

MOANING There are several types, with eight kinds of sounds: the whimper, the groan, the babble, the wail, the sigh, the shriek, the sob and words with a meaning, such as 'Mother!' 'Stop!' 'Let go!' or 'Enough!'

REVERSING ROLES There are three more methods when the roles are reversed and the woman acts the man: the 'pincer', the 'spinning top' and the 'swing'.

ORAL SEX The act consists of eight elements: the 'nominal', the 'biting the sides', the 'outer pincer', the 'inner pincer', the 'kiss', the 'lick', the 'sucking the mango' and the 'swallowing'.

SIX CHARACTERS *in* SEARCH *of an* AUTHOR

In Luigi Pirandello's postmodern play *Six Characters in Search of an Author*, which was first performed in 1921, six half-written characters interrupt a rehearsal of Pirandello's previous play *The Rules of the Game* (1918) and insist on having their unfinished story staged by the bewildered director.

The Father · The Mother · The Stepdaughter
The Son · The Boy · The Child

The CRATERS *of the* MOON

There are more than 1,500 named craters on our moon, ranging from 350 miles in diameter to a mere 30 feet. They are generally named after scientists, scholars, artists, explorers and other figures 'who have made outstanding or fundamental contributions in their field'. For example:

Aristotle · Boethius · Cyrano (de Bergerac) · Chaucer
Dante · Darwin · (Hugo) Gernsback* · Herodotus · Hesiod
Hildegard (von Bingen) · Kant · Omar Khayyam · Lucian
Lucretius · Plato · Plutarch · Marco Polo · Polybius · Seneca
Strabo · Jules Verne · H. G. Wells · Xenophon

Names for newly observed planetary features anywhere in the solar system may be suggested for the approval of the International Astronomical Union (the IAU). These literary names have all been suggested for lunar craters in the past, but sadly they were not accepted by the IAU:

Austen · Balzac · Baudelaire · Cervantes · Chekhov · Corneille
Defoe · Doyle · Dumas · Grimm · Heine · Homer · Hugo · James
Johnson · Li Po · Longfellow · Lorca · Mann · Milton · Montaigne
Montesquieu · Novalis · Pirandello · Pope · Racine · Sappho
Sophocles · Tasso · Tolstoy · Undset · Virgil · Voltaire · Zola

* Hugo Gernsback founded the first science fiction magazine – *Amazing Stories* – in 1926 and has been described as 'The Father of Science Fiction'. The World Science Fiction Convention presents annual Hugo Awards, named in his honour.

The KINGDOM *of* REDONDA

Redonda is an uninhabited rock between Antigua and Montserrat in the Leeward Islands of the Caribbean. The Montserratian novelist M. P. Shiel claimed that, at the age of fifteen, he was crowned 'King Felipe of Redonda' by an Antiguan bishop, inheriting the title from his father, who had successfully requested the island from Queen Victoria in 1865. Before he died, Shiel named the poet John Gawsworth his successor, but thereafter the line of succession becomes confused. There are at least three seemingly legitimate claimants, all of whom have granted Redondan duchies.*

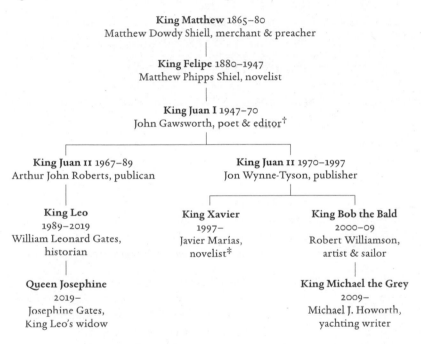

King Matthew 1865–80
Matthew Dowdy Shiell, merchant & preacher

King Felipe 1880–1947
Matthew Phipps Shiel, novelist

King Juan I 1947–70
John Gawsworth, poet & editor[†]

King Juan II 1967–89
Arthur John Roberts, publican

King Juan II 1970–1997
Jon Wynne-Tyson, publisher

King Leo
1989–2019
William Leonard Gates,
historian

King Xavier
1997–
Javier Marías,
novelist[‡]

King Bob the Bald
2000–09
Robert Williamson,
artist & sailor

Queen Josephine
2019–
Josephine Gates,
King Leo's widow

King Michael the Grey
2009–
Michael J. Howorth,
yachting writer

* The monarchs of Redonda have tended to grant titles liberally. The following authors have been raised to the Redondan peerage: William Boyd, Ray Bradbury, A. S. Byatt, J. M. Coetzee, Gerald Durrell, Lawrence Durrell, Umberto Eco, Arthur Machen, Julian MacLaren-Ross, Henry Miller, Alice Munro, Edna O'Brien, J. B. Priestley, Philip Pullman, Arthur Ransome, Dorothy L. Sayers, W. G. Sebald, Julian Symons, Dylan Thomas, John Wain and Rebecca West.

† 'John Gawsworth' was the pseudonym of Terence Armstrong, an archduke of Redonda before inheriting the crown. He wrote a biography of the author Arthur Machen, a friend of M. P. Shiel. Machen's house features in Shiel's novel *The Purple Cloud*.

‡ Since becoming King Xavier, Javier Marías has established a small publishing press called Reino de Redonda, which produces Spanish-language editions of classic texts. He writes about his succession and the history of Redonda in his self-styled 'false novel' *Dark Back of Time*.

ADULTERERS *and* ADULTERESSES

Abraham and Hagar, Ahalya and Indra, Guinevere and Lancelot – there are many archetypal adulterers, maybe because adultery represents such an emotive clash between the happiness of individuals and the expectations of society. John Updike's novel *Couples* is a high-water mark of literary infidelity: it features ten middle-class partner-swapping couples in the small town of Tarbox, Massachusetts, who engage in 'a cat's cradle of vigorous adultery', as Martin Amis puts it. Here are some more notable philanderers:

Newland Archer	*The Age of Innocence* by Edith Wharton
Edward Ashburnham	*The Good Soldier* by Ford Madox Ford
Dick Diver	*Tender is the Night* by F. Scott Fitzgerald
Edred Fitzpiers	*The Woodlanders* by Thomas Hardy
John Lewis	*That Uncertain Feeling* by Kingsley Amis*
Martin Lynch-Gibbon	*A Severed Head* by Iris Murdoch
Bobbo Patchett	*The Life and Loves of a She-Devil* by Fay Weldon
Richard Remington	*The New Machiavelli* by H. G. Wells
Henry Scobie	*The Heart of the Matter* by Graham Greene
Tomáš	*The Unbearable Lightness of Being* by Milan Kundera
Frank Wheeler	*Revolutionary Road* by Richard Yates

Ulysses by James Joyce	Molly Bloom
Madame Bovary by Gustave Flaubert	Emma Bovary (see p.49)
Effi Briest by Theodor Fontane	Effi Briest
Lady Chatterley's Lover by D. H. Lawrence	Constance Chatterley
The Painted Veil by W. Somerset Maugham	Kitty Fane
Anna Karenina by Leo Tolstoy	Anna Karenina
A Handful of Dust by Evelyn Waugh	Brenda Last
La Regenta by Leopoldo Alas	Ana Ozores
The Awakening by Kate Chopin	Edna Pontellier
The Scarlet Letter by Nathaniel Hawthorne	Hester Prynne
Thérèse Raquin by Émile Zola	Thérèse Raquin

---

* Amis was an inveterate adulterer himself. His novel *One Fat Englishman* is named after the lipstick message that his enraged first wife, Hilly Kilmarnock, daubed on his back while he was sleeping on a Yugoslav beach in 1962: '1 FAT ENGLISHMAN I FUCK ANYTHING'.

STREATFEILD'S SHOES

Noel Streatfeild is best remembered for her first children's novel, *Ballet Shoes*, about the theatrical Fossil sisters. She also wrote *Tennis Shoes*, and several of her other books have since been reissued with *Shoes* in the title.

Ballet Shoes · *Tennis Shoes* · *Circus Shoes* · *Theatre Shoes* · *Party Shoes*
Movie Shoes · *Skating Shoes* · *Family Shoes* · *Dancing Shoes* · *Travelling Shoes*

FEBRUARY HOUSE

In 1940, George Davis, the former literary editor of *Harper's Bazaar*, rented a four-storey mock-Tudor brownstone house at 7 Middagh Street in Brooklyn Heights, New York, and established an eclectic artistic commune. 'All that was new in America in music, painting or choreography emanated from that house,' said the Swiss writer Denis de Rougemont, 'the only center of thought and art I found in any large city of the country.'

RESIDENTS
W. H. Auden* · Jane Bowles* · Paul Bowles · Benjamin Britten
George Davis* · Chester Kallman · Gypsy Rose Lee
Carson McCullers* · Peter Pears · Oliver Smith*

GUESTS
Leonard Bernstein · Aaron Copland · Salvador Dalí · Denis de
Rougemont · Janet Flanner · Christopher Isherwood · Lincoln Kirstein
Lotte Lenya · Erika Mann · Golo Mann · Klaus Mann · Jerome Robbins
Solita Solano · Virgil Thomson · Kurt Weill · Richard Wright

Books written at February House include McCullers's *The Ballad of the Sad Cafe*, Auden's *The Double Man*, Jane Bowles's *Two Serious Women* and the striptease artiste Gypsy Rose Lee's *The G-String Murders*, which was a huge bestseller. The group dispersed after 1941 and the house was condemned in 1945. It was demolished to build the Brooklyn–Queens Expressway.

---

* These residents all had February birthdays, which is why Anaïs Nin (whose birthday was also in February) came up with the commune's name, 'February House'.

ON *the* ROAD

In 1946, the writer Jack Kerouac met the ex-convict Neal Cassady and the pair began making road trips across America. In April 1951, Kerouac sat down to transcribe their adventures and typed uninterruptedly for three weeks, stoked on pea soup, coffee and Benzedrine. He taped together strips of drawing paper to form a continuous, 120-foot sheet which scrolled through his typewriter: the result was a work of 'spontaneous prose', the freewheeling style for which he became known. *On the Road* was published six years later, with details of four of their extraordinary journeys.

SUMMER 1947

	Paterson, New Jersey*	
Bus to	New York City	
Hitch to	Newburgh, NY (and back)	*via* Bear Mountain, New York
Bus to	Chicago, Illinois	
Hitch to	Stuart, Iowa	*via* Davenport, Iowa
Bus to	Omaha, Nebraska	
Hitch to	Denver, Colorado	*via* Cheyenne, Wyoming
Drive to	Central City, Colorado (and back)	
Bus to	San Francisco, California	*via* Salt Lake City, Utah
Hitch to	Bakersfield, California	*via* Fresno, California
Bus to	Los Angeles, California	
Hitch to	Sabinal, California (and back)*	
Bus to	Pittsburgh, Pennsylvania	*via* Dalhart, Texas
Hitch to	New York City	*via* Harrisburg, Pennsylvania
Bus to	Paterson, New Jersey	

WINTER 1948–9

	Testament, Virginia*	
Drive to	Paterson, New Jersey (and back, twice)	*via* New York City
Drive to	New Orleans, Louisiana	*via* Macon, Georgia
Drive to	El Paso, Texas	*via* Houston, Texas
Drive to	San Francisco, California	*via* Tucson, Arizona

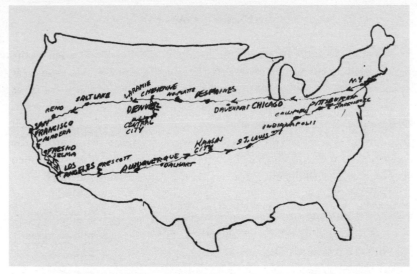

Kerouac's hand-drawn map of the first journey in *On the Road*

SPRING 1949

	Denver, Colorado	
Car-share to	San Francisco, California	*via* Salt Lake City, Utah
Car-share to	Denver, Colorado	*via* Sacramento, California
Car delivery to	Chicago, Illinois	*via* Sterling, Colorado
Bus to	Detroit, Michigan	
Car-share to	New York City	*via* Toledo, Ohio

SPRING 1950

	New York City	
Bus to	Denver, Colorado	*via* St Louis, Missouri
Drive to	San Antonio, Texas	*via* Raton, New Mexico
Drive to	Gregoria, Mexico*	*via* Laredo, Texas
Drive to	Mexico City	*via* Limon, Mexico*

* Kerouac changed some details for the 1957 edition of *On the Road*. His character, 'Sal Paradise', lives in Paterson, New Jersey, with his aunt, whereas Kerouac was actually living in Ozone Park, New York City, with his mother. Sabinal where he lives with his Mexican partner 'Terry' is really Selma, California; Testament, Virginia, was Rocky Mount, North Carolina, his sister's home; Gregoria was Ciudad Victoria in Mexico; and Llera de Canales became Limon.

The LARGEST LIBRARIES

In 'The Library of Babel', Jorge Luis Borges imagines a universe consisting of hexagonal book-lined galleries. No two books are identical, so one can calculate that the Borgesian library contains 14 billion trillion trillion books. For comparison, the largest libraries in the world are as follows:

The British Library, London	200 million items
The Library of Congress, Washington, DC	170 million items
The Shanghai Library	56 million items
The New York Public Library	55 million items
The Library and Archives Canada, Ottowa	54 million items
The Russian State Library, Moscow	48 million items
The National Diet Library, Tokyo	44 million items
The Royal Library Denmark, Copenhagen	43 million items

The NINE MUSES

In Greek mythology, the nine muses lived on Mount Helicon and inspired works of literature, science, music and the performing arts. They were the daughters of Mnemosyne, the goddess of memory. Sappho of Lesbos was sometimes called 'the tenth muse', because her poetry was so beautiful.

Calliope*	*epic poetry*
Clio	*history*
Erato	*love poetry*
Euterpe	*music*
Melpomene	*tragedy*
Polyhymnia	*hymns*
Terpsichore	*dance*
Thalia	*comedy*
Urania	*astronomy*

* Both Hesiod and Ovid considered Calliope 'the chief of all muses'. She was the mother of Orpheus, who could charm birds, beasts, trees and stones with his music.

WHY READ *the* CLASSICS?

In 1981, Italo Calvino wrote an essay in which he put forward fourteen definitions of 'classic' literature. 'It is no use reading classics out of a sense of duty or respect,' he concludes, 'we should only read them for love.'

1. The classics are those books about which you usually hear people saying: 'I'm rereading ...', never 'I'm reading ...'

2. The classics are those books which constitute a treasured experience for those who have read and loved them; but they remain just as rich an experience for those who reserve the chance to read them for when they are in the best condition to enjoy them.

3. The classics are books which exercise a particular influence, both when they imprint themselves on our imagination as unforgettable, and when they hide in the layers of memory disguised as the individual's or the collective unconscious.

4. A classic is a book which with each rereading offers as much of a sense of discovery as the first reading.

5. A classic is a book which even when we read it for the first time gives the sense of rereading something we have read before.

6. A classic is a book which has never exhausted all it has to say to its readers.

7. The classics are those books which come to us bearing the aura of previous interpretations, and trailing behind them the traces they have left in the culture or cultures (or just in the languages and customs) through which they have passed.

8. A classic is a work which constantly generates a pulviscular cloud of critical discourse around it, but which always shakes the particles off.

9. Classics are books which, the more we think we know them through hearsay, the more original, unexpected, and innovative we find them when we actually read them.

10. A classic is the term given to any book which comes to represent the whole universe, a book on a par with ancient talismans.

11. 'Your' classic is a book to which you cannot remain indifferent, and which helps you define yourself in relation or even in opposition to it.

12. A classic is a work that comes before other classics; but those who have read other classics first immediately recognize its place in the genealogy of classic works.

13. A classic is a work which relegates the noise of the present to a background hum, which at the same time the classics cannot exist without.

14. A classic is a work which persists as background noise even when a present that is totally incompatible with it holds sway.

WORKING TITLES

In Ian McEwan's *Machines Like Me*, the android Adam reads *Catch-18* by Joseph Heller, *The Last Man in Europe* by George Orwell and *All's Well that Ends Well* by Leo Tolstoy. In McEwan's alternate reality, these novels have been published under their working titles. Here are some more:

First Impressions	Jane Austen	*Pride and Prejudice*
Mistress Mary	Frances Hodgson Burnett	*The Secret Garden*
Alice's Doings in Elf-Land	Lewis Carroll	*Alice's Adventures in Wonderland*
Nobody's Fault	Charles Dickens	*Little Dorrit*
Twilight	William Faulkner	*The Sound and the Fury*
Trimalchio in West Egg	F. Scott Fitzgerald	*The Great Gatsby*
The Saddest Story	Ford Madox Ford	*The Good Soldier*
From a Sense of Duty	E. M. Forster	*Where Angels Fear to Tread*
Strangers from Within	William Golding	*Lord of the Flies*
Catch-18	Joseph Heller*	*Catch-22*
Fiesta	Ernest Hemingway	*The Sun Also Rises*
Tenderness	D. H. Lawrence	*Lady Chatterley's Lover*
Mules in Horses' Harness	Margaret Mitchell	*Gone with the Wind*
The Kingdom by the Sea	Vladimir Nabokov	*Lolita*
The Last Man in Europe	George Orwell	*Nineteen Eighty-Four*
The Strike	Ayn Rand	*Atlas Shrugged*
Prometheus Unchained	Mary Shelley	*Frankenstein* (see p.8 and p.27)
Something That Happened	John Steinbeck	*Of Mice and Men*
The Sea Cook	Robert Louis Stevenson	*Treasure Island*
The Dead Undead	Bram Stoker	*Dracula*
The War of the Ring	J. R. R. Tolkien	*The Return of the King*
All's Well That Ends Well	Leo Tolstoy	*War and Peace*
A House of the Faith	Evelyn Waugh	*Brideshead Revisited*
The Chronic Argonauts	H. G. Wells	*The Time Machine*

* Heller changed his working title after the publication of *Mila 18* by Leon Uris. 'I was heartbroken,' he said. 'I thought 18 was the only number.'

The PRECEPTS *of* POLONIUS

In *Hamlet* by William Shakespeare, Polonius prescribes his son Laertes a list of seven wise 'precepts' to bear in mind while he is at university in France.

GIVE THY THOUGHTS NO TONGUE, / Nor any unproportioned thought his act. ¶ BE THOU FAMILIAR, but by no means vulgar; / Those friends thou hast, and their adoption tried, / Grapple them to thy soul with hoops of steel; / But do not dull thy palm with entertainment / Of each new-hatched, unfledged courage. ¶ BEWARE / OF ENTRANCE TO A QUARREL, but being in, / Bear't that th'opposed may beware of thee. ¶ GIVE EVERY MAN THY EAR, but few thy voice; / Take each man's censure, but reserve thy judgement. ¶ COSTLY THY HABIT AS THY PURSE CAN BUY, / But not expressed in fancy; rich, not gaudy; / For the apparel oft proclaims the man, / And they in France of the best rank and station / Are of a most select and generous chief in that. ¶ NEITHER A BORROWER NOR A LENDER BE, / For loan oft loses both itself and friend, / And borrowing dulls the edge of husbandry. ¶ This above all: TO THINE OWN SELF BE TRUE, / And it must follow, as the night the day, / Thou canst not then be false to any man.

WAYS *of* ARRANGING ONE'S BOOKS

In 1978, Georges Perec wrote about the process of arranging and rearranging books on one's shelves, a process 'liable to produce pleasant surprises'. After discussing various locations for storing books around the house, he suggests a number of different organizational principles:

ordered ALPHABETICALLY · ordered by CONTINENT OR COUNTRY · ordered by COLOUR · ordered by DATE OF ACQUISITION · ordered by DATE OF PUBLICATION · ordered by FORMAT · ordered by GENRE · ordered by MAJOR PERIODS OF LITERARY HISTORY · ordered by LANGUAGE · ordered by PRIORITY FOR FUTURE READING · ordered by BINDING · ordered by SERIES

None of these classifications is satisfactory by itself.

Some NOMS *de* PLUME

Æ	George William Russell
Maya Angelou	Marguerite Annie Johnson
Guillaume Apollinaire	Wilhelm Albert Włodzimierz Apolinary Kostrowicki
Lewis Carroll	Charles Lutwidge Dodgson
H.D.	Hilda Doolittle
Isak Dinesen	Karen Blixen
George Eliot	Mary Ann Evans
Hans Fallada	Rudolf Wilhelm Friedrich Ditzen
C. S. Forester	Cecil Smith
Lewis Grassic Gibbon	James Leslie Mitchell
Maxim Gorky	Alexei Maximovich Peshkov
O. Henry	William Sidney Porter
Patricia Highsmith	Mary Plangman
bell hooks	Gloria Jean Watkins
Anna Kavan	Helen Woods
Jamaica Kincaid	Elaine Richardson
John le Carré	David John Moore Cornwell
Hugh MacDiarmid	Christopher Murray Grieve
André Maurois	Émile Herzog
Yukio Mishima	Kimitake Hiraoka
Molière	Jean-Baptiste Poquelin
Toni Morrison	Chloe Wofford
Pablo Neruda	Ricardo Eliécer Neftalí Reyes Basoalto
Novalis	Georg Philipp Friedrich Freiherr von Hardenberg
Flann O'Brien	Brian O'Nolan
George Orwell	Eric Arthur Blair
Premchand	Dhanpat Rai Srivastav
Ayn Rand	Alisa Zinovyevna Rosenbaum
Jean Rhys	Gwen Williams
Saki	Hector Hugh Munro
George Sand	Amandine Lucie Aurore Dupin
Stendhal	Marie-Henri Beyle
Italo Svevo	Aron Ettore Schmitz
Mark Twain	Samuel Langhorne Clemens
Voltaire	François-Marie Arouet
Rebecca West	Cicily Fairfield

The TYPES of READER

'Readers may be divided into four classes,' said Samuel Taylor Coleridge, in a lecture on the subject of poetry that he delivered in November 1811:

I. SPONGES, who absorb all they read, and return it nearly in the same state, only a little dirtied.
II. SAND-GLASSES, who retain nothing, and are content to get through a book for the sake of getting through the time.
III. STRAIN-BAGS, who retain merely the dregs of what they read.
IV. MOGUL DIAMONDS, equally rare and valuable, who profit by what they read, and enable others to profit by it also.

Some UNUSUAL PETS

Virgil is said to have held a funeral for his pet fly, and may have written a poem about a gnat's grave. Many other authors have had unusual pets.

Bruin	a bear*	Lord Byron
Dindiki	a potto†	André Gide
Diogenes	a vulture	Alexandre Dumas
Edward	a myna bird	Hunter S. Thompson
Henry Ford	a cockerel	George Orwell
Kiria	a mongoose	Pablo Neruda
Minerva	an owl	Karen Blixen
Miss Kong	a monkey	Arthur C. Clarke
Mitz	a marmoset	Leonard & Virginia Woolf
Peaky	a peacock	Edith Sitwell
Thibault	a lobster‡	Gérard de Nerval
Top	a wombat	Dante Gabriel Rossetti

* When Byron arrived as a student at Cambridge, he wasn't able to bring his bulldog Smut, so he bought a bear at Stourbridge Fair and kept it in his rooms. (For another of his dogs, see p.17.)
† Pottos are nocturnal sloth-like tailless primates from central Africa, sometimes called 'softly-softlies'. Gide fed Dindiki a diet of jam and condensed milk.
‡ Nerval once took Thibault for a walk in the Palais-Royal gardens in Paris.

The earliest printer's mark appeared in 1457, a few years after Gutenberg established movable type printing in Mainz (see p.124). Commissioned by Johann Fust and his son-in-law Peter Schöffer, it consisted of a pair of twin shields hanging from a branch. Since then, publishers have often chosen an emblem or 'colophon' to identify their books. The book in your hands, for example, has an origami rabbit on the title page, which is the emblem of Particular Books, an imprint of Penguin. Here are some more examples:

Little, Brown & Co.
1837
The Charles Bulfinch
memorial in Boston

Chatto & Windus
1855
Two reading
cherubs

William Heinemann
1890
A windmill, designed
by William Nicholson

Doubleday
1897
A dolphin wrapped
around an anchor

Alfred A. Knopf
1915
A borzoi*

Jonathan Cape
1921
A vase of fruit

Simon & Schuster
1924
A sower, designed by
John Everett Millais

Viking
1925
A Viking longship†

Random House
1927
Candide's house, with
its well-tended garden‡

Faber & Faber
1929
Two Fs, although there
was no second Faber,
only Geoffrey Faber

Hamish Hamilton
1931
An oak tree growing
out of a book

Penguin Books
1935
A penguin, considered
'dignified but flippant'
by founder Allen Lane

Pan Books
1944
Pan, based on a drawing
by Mervyn Peake

Harvill Press
1946
A leopard, based on the
cover of *The Leopard* by
Giuseppe di Lampedusa

Farrar, Straus & Giroux
1960
Three fish, borrowed
from the German
publisher Fischer Verlag

Bloomsbury
1986
Diana, goddess of the hunt

HarperCollins
1989
Fire and water§

Particular Books
2009
An origami rabbit

---

* A borzoi is a Russian wolfhound. Alfred Knopf's wife Blanche chose it because she thought of
borzois as a 'regally dignified, loyal and affectionate' breed. She subsequently owned borzois
and found them to be 'cowardly, stupid, disloyal and full of self-pity'.

† The publisher Harold Guinzburg planned to name his company the Half Moon Press, after
the Dutch flyboat on which Henry Hudson sailed to what is now New York. Guinzburg
commissioned a drawing of the boat from the artist Rockwell Kent, but Kent delivered an
image of a Viking *drakkar* instead, so Guinzburg changed the name of the company.

‡ *Candide* by Voltaire was the first title published by Random House, a firm set up to publish
'a few books on the side at random'. The colophon is based on Rockwell Kent's illustration
of the 'small farm' where Candide retires at the end of the book.

§ HarperCollins was formed from the 1989 merger of Harper & Row (1817) and William Collins
(1819). Harper's colophon was a flaming torch and Collins's was a water fountain, so the new
logo combines both elements.

The STATE *of* MY AFFAIRS

When the mariner Robinson Kreutznaer, known as Crusoe, is shipwrecked on a desert island off the coast of Venezuela – in the novel *Robinson Crusoe* by Daniel Defoe – he starts by constructing living quarters and then takes stock of his circumstances. Close to despair, he decides to set his comforts against his misfortunes in the manner of a double-entry account book. Surprisingly, this exercise turns out in favour of 'the credit side of the accompt' and affords Crusoe a modicum of 'relish' for his solitary state.

EVIL	GOOD
I am cast upon a horrible, desolate island, void of all hope of recovery.	But I am alive, and not drown'd, as all my ship's company was.
I am singled out and separated, as it were, from all the world to be miserable.	But I am singled out too from all the ship's crew to be spared from death; and he that miraculously saved me from death, can deliver me from this condition.
I am divided from mankind, a solitaire, one banish'd from human society.	But I am not starv'd and perishing on a barren place, affording no sustenance.
I have no clothes to cover me.	But I am in a hot climate, where if I had clothes I could hardly wear them.
I am without any defence or means to resist any violence of man or beast.	But I am cast on an island, where I see no wild beasts to hurt me, as I saw on the coast of *Africa*: and what if I had been shipwreck'd there?
I have no soul to speak to, or relieve me.	But God wonderfully sent the ship in near enough to the shore, that I have gotten out so many necessary things as will either supply my wants, or enable me to supply my self, even as long as I live.

The RIGHTS *of the* READER

'You can't make someone read,' says the French author Daniel Pennac. 'Just as you can't make them fall in love, or dream...' In 1992, Pennac wrote *The Rights of the Reader*, a celebration of the art of reading, and he distilled his book into the following ten-point manifesto:

The right not to read. ¶ The right to skip. ¶ The right not to finish a book. ¶ The right to read it again. ¶ The right to read anything. ¶ The right to mistake a book for real life. ¶ The right to read anywhere. ¶ The right to dip in. ¶ The right to read out loud. ¶ The right to be quiet.

The LIMITS *of* SHERLOCK HOLMES

In *A Study in Scarlet*, Dr John Watson is surprised to learn that his otherwise brilliant fellow lodger at 221B Baker Street has no idea that the Earth orbits the Sun. He decides to review the limits of this curious man's knowledge.

1. Knowledge of Literature. – Nil.
2. Philosophy. – Nil.
3. Astronomy. – Nil.
4. Politics. – Feeble.
5. Botany. – Variable. Well up in belladonna, opium, and poisons generally. Knows nothing of practical gardening.
6. Geology. – Practical, but limited. Tells at a glance different soils from each other. After walks has shown me splashes upon his trousers, and told me by their colour and consistence in what part of London he had received them.
7. Chemistry. – Profound.
8. Anatomy. – Accurate, but unsystematic.
9. Sensational Literature. – Immense. He appears to know every detail of every horror perpetrated in the century.
10. Plays the violin well.
11. Is an expert singlestick player, boxer, and swordsman.
12. Has a good practical knowledge of British law.

HERE BE MONSTERS

'He who fights with monsters should be careful lest he thereby become a monster,' warned Friedrich Nietzsche in *Beyond Good and Evil*. Here are some of the most gruesome monsters in literature:

Apollyon	'had wings like a dragon, and feet like a bear, and out of his belly came fire and smoke'	*The Pilgrim's Progress* by John Bunyan
Behemoth	'an enormous black cat with a cavalry moustache, that walks on two legs'	*The Master and Margarita* by Mikhail Bulgakov
Count Dracula	'sharp white teeth [...] extraordinary pallor'	*Dracula* by Bram Stoker
The Creature	'yellow skin scarcely covered the work of muscles and arteries beneath'	*Frankenstein* by Mary Shelley
Grendel	'shadow-stalker, stealthy and swift'	*Beowulf*
Humbaba	'A tempest's onslaught is ferocious Humbaba!'	*The Epic of Gilgamesh*
The Jabberwock	'jaws that bite [...] claws that catch'	*Through the Looking-Glass* by Lewis Carroll
The Kraken	'a horned beak like a parrot's, opened and shut vertically'	*Twenty Thousand Leagues Under the Sea* by Jules Verne
The Loch Ness Monster	'the monster [...] giving an awful roar, darted after him, with its mouth wide open'	*The Life of St Columba* by Adomnán of Iona
Scylla	'six long scrawny necks, each ending in a grisly head with triple rows of fangs'	*The Odyssey* by Homer
Shelob	'an evil thing in spider-form [...] weaving webs of shadow'	*The Lord of the Rings* by J. R. R. Tolkien
Shoggoth	'a shapeless congeries of protoplasmic bubbles, faintly self-luminous, and with myriads of temporary eyes forming and un-forming as pustules of greenish light'	*At the Mountains of Madness* by H. P. Lovecraft

STUCK *in the* MIDDLE

Some authors prefer to use their middle name:

(*Helen*) Beatrix Potter • (*Samuel*) Dashiell Hammett
(*Mary*) Flannery O'Connor • (*Henry*) Graham Greene • (*Nelle*) Harper Lee
(*Giles*) Lytton Strachey • (*Clarence*) Malcolm Lowry
(*Joseph*) Rudyard Kipling • (*Harry*) Sinclair Lewis • (*William*) Somerset
Maugham • (*Percy*) Wyndham Lewis • (*Adeline*) Virginia Woolf

The INDOMITABLE GAULS

The *Asterix* comics by René Goscinny and Albert Uderzo describe the
adventures of a small group of Gauls who hold out against the Romans
with the aid of a magic strengthening potion. The names of the principal
characters are puns on French words and phrases, and translators have had
fun finding similar puns when putting the comics into other languages.

Astérix	*astérisque**	the Gaul	Asterix
Obélix	*obélisque*	Asterix's friend	Obelix[†]
Idéfix	*idée fixe*	Obelix's dog	Dogmatix
Panoramix	*panorama*	the druid	Getafix
Abraracourcix	*à bras raccoucis*[‡]	the village chief	Vitalstatistix
Bonnemine	*bonne mine*	the chief's wife	Impedimenta
Assurancetourix	*assurance tous risques*	the bard	Cacofonix
Agecanonix	*âge canonique*	the village elder	Geriatrix
Ordralfabétix	*ordre alphabétique*	the fishmonger	Unhygienix
Iélosubmarine	'Yellow Submarine'	the fishmonger's wife	Bacteria
Cétautomatix	*c'est automatique*	the blacksmith	Fulliautomatix

* See p.18.
† *Asterix* was translated into English by Anthea Bell, the award-winning translator of Franz
Kafka and W. G. Sebald. Her 'ingenious translations' of the names, says the critic Peter Hunt,
'display the art of the translator at its best'.
‡ The chief's French name is a reference to the idiomatic phrase *tomber sur quelqu'un à bras
raccourcis*, which literally means 'to fall on someone with short arms', but has the sense of
attacking violently.

FROM *the* LIBRARY *of*

A bookplate or 'ex libris' is a slip of paper, pasted into a book, which identifies its owner. The earliest known example dates from 1480. Originally the preserve of wealthy private library owners, from the nineteenth century it became increasingly fashionable to commission one's own ex libris, and several authors have used personalized bookplates over the years.

Aldous Huxley

H. P. Lovecraft

Elizabeth von Arnim

Sigmund Freud

Robert Frost
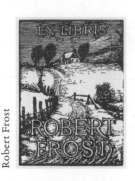

Ernest Hemingway

H. G. Wells

Rudyard Kipling

Jack London

WEIRD LITTLE MARKS

'There's no need to blot the page up with weird little marks,' says Cormac McCarthy. 'I mean, if you write properly you shouldn't have to punctuate.' Here are some other authors' views on punctuation marks:

; **SEMICOLONS** 'First rule: Do not use semicolons. They are transvestite hermaphrodites representing absolutely nothing. All they do is show you've been to college.' — Kurt Vonnegut

, **COMMAS** 'Commas are servile [...] A comma by helping you along holding your coat for you and putting on your shoes keeps you from living your life as actively as you should lead it.' — Gertrude Stein

" **INVERTED COMMAS** 'Perverted commas.' — James Joyce "

' **APOSTROPHES** 'There is not the faintest reason for persisting in the ugly and silly trick of peppering pages with these uncouth bacilli.' — George Bernard Shaw

? **QUESTION MARKS** 'Positively revolting.' — Gertrude Stein

! **EXCLAMATION MARKS** 'An exclamation point is like laughing at your own joke.' — F. Scott Fitzgerald

The DETECTION CLUB

Founded in 1930, the Detection Club is a group of British mystery writers. Initially, members had to abide by Ronald Knox's 'Rules of Fair Play' (see p.131) and swear by oath to forgo plots that rely on 'Divine Revelation, Feminine Intuition, Mumbo Jumbo, Jiggery-Pokery, Coincidence, or Act of God'. The club has produced several co-authored books, such as *Behind the Screen* and *The Floating Admiral*. There have been nine presidents so far, including E. C. Bentley, inventor of the clerihew (see p.42):

G. K. Chesterton • E. C. Bentley • Dorothy L. Sayers
Agatha Christie • Lord Gorell • Julian Symons • H. R. F. Keating
Simon Brett • Martin Edwards *(current)*

RULES *for* WRITING

'The great enemy of clear language is insincerity,' wrote George Orwell in his essay 'Politics and the English Language'. 'When there is a gap between one's real and one's declared aims, one turns as it were instinctively to long words and exhausted idioms, like a cuttlefish spurting out ink.' In the same essay, he set out six rules for writing good English:

   i. Never use a metaphor, simile or other figure of speech which you are used to seeing in print.
  ii. Never use a long word where a short one will do.
 iii. If it is possible to cut a word out, always cut it out.
 iv. Never use the passive where you can use the active.
  v. Never use a foreign phrase, a scientific word or a jargon word if you can think of an everyday English equivalent.
 vi. Break any of these rules sooner than say anything outright barbarous.

The LOST GENERATION

'You are all a lost generation,' said Gertrude Stein to Ernest Hemingway, who used the line as an epigraph to his novel *The Sun Also Rises* (see p.50). Stein had heard a French mechanic using the phrase *génération perdue* while her car was being serviced, and the term came to apply to a group of young American writers, disillusioned by the First World War and adrift without moral bearings in Paris. Lost Generation writers include:

Djuna Barnes • Sylvia Beach • Malcolm Cowley* • Hart Crane
e e cummings • John Dos Passos • T. S. Eliot • William Faulkner • F. Scott
Fitzgerald • Ernest Hemingway • Edna St Vincent Millay • Henry Miller
Ezra Pound • Gertrude Stein • Thornton Wilder • Thomas Wolfe

* Before Malcolm Cowley became an editor at the Viking Press (see p.82), and transformed the careers of William Faulkner, Jack Kerouac and Ken Kesey, he lived in Paris and wrote poetry. He later wrote a definitive account of the Lost Generation called *Exile's Return*. Hemingway described Cowley as 'that American poet with a pile of saucers in front of him and a stupid look on his potato face talking about the Dada movement'.

The BOOKS YOU HAVEN'T READ

In the opening chapter of *If on a winter's night a traveller*, Italo Calvino described how you, the reader, went to a bookshop to buy your copy of *If on a winter's night a traveller*. He presented the experience as a military manoeuvre, in which you had to battle your way past an imposing list of 'Books You Haven't Read' before you could reach the till. These include:

Books You Needn't Read
Books Made For Purposes Other Than Reading
Books Read Even Before You Open Them Since They Belong To The
    Category Of Books Read Before Being Written
Books That If You Had More Than One Life You Would Certainly Also
    Read But Unfortunately Your Days Are Numbered
Books You Mean To Read But There Are Others You Must Read First
Books Too Expensive Now And You'll Wait Till They're Remaindered
Books ditto When They Come Out In Paperback
Books You Can Borrow From Somebody
Books That Everybody's Read So It's As If You Had Read Them, Too
Books You've Been Planning To Read For Ages
Books You've Been Hunting For Years Without Success
Books Dealing With Something You're Working On At The Moment
Books You Want To Own So They'll Be Handy Just In Case
Books You Could Put Aside Maybe To Read This Summer
Books You Need To Go With Other Books On Your Shelves
Books That Fill You With Sudden, Inexplicable Curiosity, Not Easily
    Justified
Books Read Long Ago Which It's Now Time to Reread
Books You've Always Pretended to Have Read And Now It's Time
    to Sit Down And Really Read Them (see p.77)
New Books Whose Author Or Subject Appeals To You
New Books By Authors Or On Subjects Not New (for you or in general)
New Books By Authors Or On Subjects Completely Unknown
    (at least to you)

Once you bought your copy of *If on a winter's night a traveller*, however, the other books ceased to be intimidating. As you left, they looked at you 'with the bewildered gaze of dogs who, from their cages in the city pound, see a former companion go off on the leash of his master'.

The MUSIC of DYSTOPIA

Stanley Kubrick's film version of A *Clockwork Orange* features an electronic soundtrack by Wendy Carlos, who adapts classical music by Beethoven and Rossini. Several musicians have been inspired by dystopian texts:

GEORGE ORWELL'S *NINETEEN EIGHTY-FOUR*

Who Are You?	Black Sabbath
1984	David Bowie
Doublethink	Douglas Dare
Sexcrime	Eurythmics
Standards	The Jam
Restless	Elton John
United Sates of Eurasia	Muse
2 + 2 = 5	Radiohead
Two Minutes of Hate	SHVPES
Big Brother	Subhumans
Doublespeak	Thrice
Winston Smith Takes It on the Jaw	Utopia
Big Brother	Stevie Wonder

ANTHONY BURGESS'S *A CLOCKWORK ORANGE*

Looking Down the Barrel of a Gun	Beastie Boys
Agent Orange	Cage
Drencrom Velocet Synthemesc	Campag Velocet
Ultraviolence	Lana Del Rey
A Clockwork Orange	Rancid
Horrorshow	Scars
Moloko Mesto	Sepultura
Hier Kommt Alex	Die Toten Hosen

ALDOUS HUXLEY'S *BRAVE NEW WORLD*

I Have Seen the Future	The Bravery
Brave New World	Iron Maiden
Brave New World	Kalandra
Soma	The Strokes

METRICAL FEET

A poem's 'metre' is a combination of the number of 'feet' in each line and their pattern of stressed or unstressed syllables. The most common metre in English poetry is iambic pentameter: five feet of two syllables per line, with second syllables stressed. Shakespeare and Milton wrote in unrhymed lines of iambic pentameter known as 'blank verse'.

˘ ˘	pyrrhus	*pyrrhic*	('in a')
˘ –	iamb	*iambic*	('toDAY')
– ˘	trochee	*trochaic*	('LOVer')
– –	spondee	*spondaic*	('BOOKMARK')
˘ ˘ ˘	tribrach	*tribrachic*	('and in the')
– ˘ ˘	dactyl	*dactylic*	('FELLOwship')
˘ – ˘	amphibrach	*amphibrachic*	('eTERNal')
˘ ˘ –	anapaest	*anapaestic*	('underSTAND')
˘ – –	bacchius	*bacchiac*	('at DAY BREAK')
– ˘ –	amphimacer	*cretic*	('PIECE of CAKE')
– – ˘	antibacchius	*antibacchiac*	('RED LETTer')
– – –	molossus	*molossic*	('NO BIRDS SING')

NUMBER OF FEET

monometer (1 foot) • *dimeter* (2 feet) • *trimeter* (3 feet)
tetrameter (4 feet) • *pentameter* (5 feet) • *hexameter* (6 feet)
heptameter (7 feet) • *octameter* (8 feet)

A TRILOGY *in* FIVE PARTS

The Hitch Hiker's Guide to the Galaxy
The Restaurant at the End of the Universe • Life, the Universe and Everything
*So Long, and Thanks for All the Fish • Mostly Harmless**

* Douglas Adams died in 2001, before he could add a sixth instalment to his trilogy, but in 2009 Eoin Colfer published *And Another Thing …* on the thirtieth anniversary of the original novel.

The **TREE-ALPHABET** *of the* **DRUIDS**

The earliest records of the Irish language are written in Ogham, sometimes known as the 'language of the druids' or the 'tree-alphabet', because each letter is named after a tree or woodland plant. Ogham inscriptions are written vertically and read from bottom to top: the script emerged in the fourth century AD and remained in use until the eighteenth.

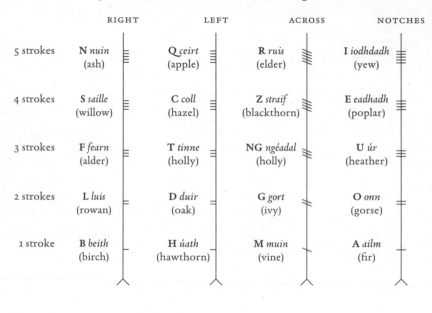

	RIGHT	LEFT	ACROSS	NOTCHES
5 strokes	**N** *nuin* (ash)	**Q** *ceirt* (apple)	**R** *ruis* (elder)	**I** *iodhdadh* (yew)
4 strokes	**S** *saille* (willow)	**C** *coll* (hazel)	**Z** *straif* (blackthorn)	**E** *eadhadh* (poplar)
3 strokes	**F** *fearn* (alder)	**T** *tinne* (holly)	**NG** *ngéadal* (holly)	**U** *úr* (heather)
2 strokes	**L** *luis* (rowan)	**D** *duir* (oak)	**G** *gort* (ivy)	**O** *onn* (gorse)
1 stroke	**B** *beith* (birch)	**H** *úath* (hawthorn)	**M** *muin* (vine)	**A** *ailm* (fir)

Some **MIDDLE INITIALS**

In 2014, researchers at Southampton University showed that authors who use a middle initial are perceived as better writers than those who don't.

Robert A(*nson*) Heinlein · Arthur C(*harles*) Clarke · Philip K(*indred*) Dick
Jerome K(*lapka*) Jerome · Ursula K(*roeber*) Le Guin · James M(*allahan*) Cain
Iain M(*enzies*) Banks · George R(*aymond*) R(*ichard*) Martin
William S(*eward*) Burroughs · Hunter S(*tockton*) Thompson
Pearl S(*ydenstricker*) Buck · James T(*homas*) Farrell

The USELESS CHRISTMAS PRESENTS

In *A Child's Christmas in Wales*, Dylan Thomas recalled the glorious snowy Christmases of his boyhood. 'I can never remember whether it snowed for six days and six nights when I was twelve,' he wrote, 'or whether it snowed for twelve days and twelve nights when I was six.' After describing the 'useful' presents he received at Christmas – mufflers, mittens, scarves, etc. – he moved on to the glorious 'Useless Presents':

Bags of moist and many-coloured jelly babies
and a folded flag
and a false nose
and a tram-conductor's cap and a machine that punched tickets
    and rang a bell;
never a catapult;
once, by a mistake that no one could explain, a little hatchet;
and a celluloid duck that made, when you pressed it, a most
    unducklike sound, a mewing moo that an ambitious cat might
    make who wished to be a cow;
and a painting book in which I could make the grass, the trees,
    the sea and the animals any colour I pleased, and still the dazzling
    sky-blue sheep are grazing in the red field under the rainbow-
    billed and pea-green birds.
Hard-boileds, toffee, fudge and allsorts, crunches, cracknels,
    humbugs, glaciers, marzipan, and butterwelsh for the Welsh.
And troops of bright tin soldiers who, if they could not fight,
    could always run.
And Snakes-and-Families and Happy Ladders.
And Easy Hobbi-Games for Little Engineers, complete with
    instructions. Oh, easy for Leonardo!
And a whistle to make the dogs bark to wake up the old man next
    door to make him beat on the wall with his stick to shake our
    picture off the wall.
And a packet of cigarettes: you put one in your mouth and you stood
    at the corner of the street and you waited for hours, in vain, for
    an old lady to scold you for smoking a cigarette, and then with
    a smirk you ate it.
And then it was breakfast under the balloons.

TWELVE NOTES *on the* MYSTERY STORY

Raymond Chandler drew up this list in 1948 (see also p.131). 'Modern detective stories fall into seven loose classifications,' he observed elsewhere: '(1) the deductive story (clues and deducing), (2) the tough school (gore, sex and four-letter words), (3) the had-I-but-known, (4) the old maid school-teacher detective (the lace panties story), (5) the locked-room murder method, (6) the fast-action thriller, (7) the screwball, anything goes story.'

1. It must be credibly motivated, both as to the original situation and the denouement.
2. It must be technically sound as to the methods of murder and detection.
3. It must be honest with the reader.
4. It must be realistic as to character, setting, and atmosphere.
5. It must have a sound story value apart from the mystery element.
6. To achieve this it must have some form of suspense, even if only intellectual.
7. It must have color, lift, and a reasonable amount of dash.
8. It must have enough essential simplicity to be explained easily when the time comes. (This is possibly the most often violated of all the rules.)
9. It must baffle a reasonably intelligent reader.
10. The solution must seem inevitable once revealed.
11. It must not try to do everything at once.
12. It must punish the criminal in one way or another, not necessarily by operation of the law.

The INKLINGS

Founded in 1933, the Inklings were a loose group of Oxford academics, who met in Magdalen College and The Eagle and Child pub to discuss literature and read from works in progress. Regular members included:

Owen Barfield · Lord David Cecil · Nevill Coghill
Hugo Dyson · Adam Fox · C. S. Lewis · Christopher Tolkien
J. R. R. Tolkien · John Wain · Charles Williams

BOWIE'S BOOKS

In 2013, two years before his death, David Bowie compiled a list of 100 books that had influenced him, for the *David Bowie Is* exhibition in Toronto. Most of the books on his list were written during his lifetime, but twenty-six were published before he was born in 1947:

The Portable Dorothy Parker / Dorothy Parker

Mr Norris Changes Trains / Christopher Isherwood

Les Chants de Maldoror / Comte de Lautréamont

The Road to Wigan Pier / George Orwell

Lady Chatterley's Lover / D. H. Lawrence

Berlin Alexanderplatz / Alfred Döblin

The Day of the Locust / Nathanael West

Infants of the Spring / Wallace Thurman*

The Great Gatsby / F. Scott Fitzgerald

The 42nd Parallel / John Dos Passos

Madame Bovary / Gustave Flaubert

As I Lay Dying / William Faulkner

Transcendental Magic, Its Doctrine and Ritual / Eliphas Lévi

English Journey / J. B. Priestley

The Outsider / Albert Camus

The Waste Land / T. S. Eliot

BLAST / ed. Wyndham Lewis

Zanoni / Edward Bulwer Lytton

Vile Bodies / Evelyn Waugh

The Bridge / Hart Crane

McTeague / Frank Norris

Black Boy / Richard Wright

Inferno / Dante Alighieri

The Street / Ann Petry

Passing / Nella Larsen*

The Iliad / Homer

* See p.112

DICKENS' VILLAINS

Charles Dickens loved the theatre, and had a talent for portraying melo-dramatic villains in his novels. Here are some of the most dastardly:

JAMES CARKER, a company manager	*Dombey and Son*
SIR JOHN CHESTER, a gentleman	*Barnaby Rudge*
COMPEYSON, a conman	*Great Expectations*
MME. DEFARGE, a tricoteuse	*A Tale of Two Cities*
URIAH HEEP, a lawyer's clerk	*David Copperfield*
SETH PECKSNIFF, an architect	*Martin Chuzzlewit*
DANIEL QUILP, a moneylender	*The Old Curiosity Shop*
M. RIGAUD, a blackmailer	*Little Dorrit*
BILL SIKES, a housebreaker	*Oliver Twist*
WACKFORD SQUEERS, a schoolmaster	*Nicholas Nickleby*

NOBEL NON-LAUREATES

Since 1901, the annual Nobel Prize for Literature has been the world's most esteemed literary prize, but it is only awarded to living authors, so there have been many notable non-winners, including the following:

Chinua Achebe • W. H. Auden • Simone de Beauvoir • Jorge Luis Borges*
Bertolt Brecht • F. Scott Fitzgerald • E. M. Forster† • Robert Frost
Graham Greene • Thomas Hardy • Aldous Huxley • Henrik Ibsen
Eugène Ionesco • Henry James • James Joyce • Jack Kerouac
Federico García Lorca • Yukio Mishima • Vladimir Nabokov
George Orwell • Marcel Proust • Leo Tolstoy • H. G. Wells
Edith Wharton • Thornton Wilder • Virginia Woolf • Émile Zola

---

* 'Not granting me the Nobel Prize has become a Scandinavian tradition,' joked Borges; 'since I was born they have not been granting it to me.' *The Economist* once said that Borges was 'probably the greatest twentieth-century author never to win the Nobel Prize'.

† Each year, the Swedish Academy considers nominations sent in by academics, literary organizations and former Nobel laureates. The nominations are kept secret for fifty years. We now know, for example, that Thomas Hardy was nominated in twelve different years without winning; Graham Greene at least fifteen times; and E. M. Forster twenty times.

A USER'S MANUAL

Life A User's Manual, Georges Perec's masterpiece, is a novel, a jigsaw puzzle, a chess match and a game of go. It describes a fictional apartment block, 11 rue Simon-Crubellier, in the 17th arrondissement in Paris: the block has ten floors of ten rooms and one chapter devoted to each room. The book follows a 'knight's tour' around this 10 × 10 grid: moving from room to room in the manner of a chess knight, visiting each one once. 'It will be noticed,' said Perec, 'that the book has 99, not 100 chapters. The little girl who appears on pages 231 and 318 is entirely responsible for this.' The missing chapter (and room) is the corner cellar between chapters 65 and 66. This is a 'clinamen', Perec's deliberate swerving of his own rules. The girl he mentions is a picture on a biscuit tin at the end of chapter 65: she nibbles the corner off a *petit beurre* and off the corner of the grid.

Honoré						*Morellet*	*Simpson Troyan Troquet*		
59	83	15	10	57	48	7	52	45	54
		Smautf	Sutton	Orlowska	Albin			Plassaert	
						Jérôme	*Fresnel*		
97	11	58	82	16	9	46	55	6	51
Hutting		Gratiolet		Crespi	Nieto & Rogers			Breidel	Valène
Brodin–Gratiolet								*Jérôme*	
84	60	96	14	47	56	49	8	53	44
Cinoc		Doctor Dinteville						Winckler	
Hourcade		*Gratiolet*	*Grifalconi*					*Hérbert*	
12	98	81	86	95	17	28	43	50	5
Réol								Foulerot	
Speiss								*Echard*	
61	85	13	18	27	79	94	4	41	30
Berger		Rorschach			Stairs			Marquiseaux	
		Danglars						*Colomb*	
99	70	26	80	87	1	42	29	93	3
		Bartlebooth						Foureau	
		Appenzzell							
25	62	88	69	19	36	78	2	31	40
		Altamont						De Beaumont	
71	65	20	23	89	68	34	37	77	92
		Moreau						Louvet	
				Claveau				*Massy*	
63	24	66	73	35	22	90	75	39	32
Service Entrance		Marcia, Antiques		Office Nochère	Entrance Hall			Marcia	
	72	64	21	67	74	38	33	91	76
Cellars		Boiler Room	Cellars		Lift Machinery			Cellars	

99

BOND MOVES *and* MATES

In his essay 'The Narrative Structure in Fleming', Umberto Eco described the 'invariable scheme' of Ian Fleming's James Bond novels as a sequence of chess moves. (For another book based on chess moves, see p.146.)

A. M moves and gives a task to Bond.
B. The Villain moves and appears to Bond (perhaps in alternating forms).
C. Bond moves and gives a first check to the Villain or the Villain gives first check to Bond.
D. Woman moves and shows herself to Bond.
E. Bond consumes Woman: possesses her or begins her seduction.
F. The Villain captures Bond (with or without Woman, or at different moments).
G. The Villain tortures Bond (with or without Woman).
H. Bond conquers the Villain (kills him, or kills his representative or helps at their killing).
I. Bond convalescing enjoys Woman, whom he then loses.

LIBRARIES *on the* INSIDE

In the dystopian world of *Fahrenheit 451** by Ray Bradbury, it is illegal to read books, which are routinely incinerated, but an informal organization of human 'dust jackets' has emerged, each of whom memorizes an author's works to keep them safe for future generations. They are 'bums on the outside, libraries inside'. The writers they have internalized include:

Aristophanes · Marcus Aurelius · Gautama Buddha · Lord Byron
Confucius · Charles Darwin · Albert Einstein · the Evangelists
Mahatma Gandhi · Thomas Hardy · Thomas Jefferson · Abraham Lincoln
Niccolò Machiavelli · José Ortega y Gasset · Thomas Paine
Thomas Love Peacock · Plato · Bertrand Russell · Arthur Schopenhauer
Albert Schweitzer · Jonathan Swift · Henry David Thoreau

---

* The title *Fahrenheit 451* is 'the temperature at which book paper catches fire and burns'. In fact, paper burns at 451° Celsius, but Bradbury thought that Fahrenheit sounded better.

AROUND *the* WORLD *in* EIGHTY DAYS

In 1872, Thomas Cook advertised the first round-the-world tour, which lasted seven months. In Jules Verne's novel of the same year, Phileas Fogg wagers £20,000 that he can circle the globe in just eighty days, returning to the Reform Club on Pall Mall before 8.45 p.m. on 21 December.

2–5 Oct	London → Paris → Turin → Brindisi	train & ferry	3 days
5–20 Oct	Brindisi → Suez → Aden → Bombay	steamer	15 days
20–25 Oct	Bombay → Allahabad → Calcutta	train & elephant*	5 days
25 Oct– 6 Nov	Calcutta → Singapore → Hong Kong	steamer	12 days
6–7 Nov	Hong Kong	(stopover)	1 day
7–11 Nov	Hong Kong → Shanghai	pilot boat	4 days
11 Nov– 3 Dec	Shanghai → Yokohama → San Francisco	steamer	22 days
3–8 Dec†	San Francisco → Salt Lake City → Fort Kearney	train	5 days
9 Dec	Fort Kearney → Omaha	a sledge with sails‡	1 day
9–11 Dec	Omaha → Chicago → New York	train	2 days
11–12 Dec	New York	(stopover)	1 day
12–20 Dec	New York → Queenstown	steamer	8 days
21 Dec	Queenstown → Dublin → Liverpool → London	train & ferry	1 day

* Fogg bases his bet on an article in the *Daily Telegraph*, which reports on a new railway line built from Bombay to Calcutta. When he gets there, however, Fogg discovers that a fifty-mile section of this line – from Kholby to Allahabad – is not yet built, so he buys an elephant.

† These and the following dates are assumed by Fogg. As he is travelling east, he 'loses' four minutes with every degree of longitude he passes, meaning that he experiences eighty days and nights when seventy-nine days have passed in London. He discovers this fact only in the final chapter, but he might have realized sooner, because having passed what is now the international date line in the Pacific Ocean, the date on his arrival in San Francisco would have been 2 December, not the 3rd.

‡ Fogg misses the train from Fort Kearney because his servant Passepartout is temporarily captured by a Sioux tribe. He manages to engage the services of a man called Mudge, who drives a 'curious vehicle' with sledge runners and a large sail. By this means, he travels 200 miles in five hours across the snowy Nebraskan prairie. This is his most unusual mode of transport; unlike David Niven in the 1956 film, Fogg never takes a hot air balloon.

DESERT ISLAND BOOKS

The BBC Radio programme *Desert Island Discs* has been running since 1942; in each episode, a guest is invited to choose the musical tracks they would want if they were marooned on a desert island. Since 1951 they have also been given the Bible and the complete works of Shakespeare, and one other book. These are the ten most popular choices:

> a poetry anthology • an encyclopaedia • *In Search of Lost Time*
> by Marcel Proust • a dictionary • *War and Peace* by Leo Tolstoy
> a blank book • a survival manual • *The Decline and Fall of the*
> *Roman Empire* by Edward Gibbon • a dictionary of quotations
> *The Lord of the Rings* by J. R. R. Tolkien

The FALSE SPINES of CHARLES DICKENS

Dickens commissioned the bookbinder Thomas Robert Eeles to construct fake bookshelves for his study, providing long lists of invented titles to be embossed in leather on the false book spines. Here is a small selection:

Noah's *Arkitecture*. 2 vols.
The Art of Cutting the Teeth.
Five Minutes in China. 3 vols.
Hansard's *Guide to Refreshing Sleep*. As many volumes as possible.
History of a Short Chancery Law Suit. 20 vols.
Cat's *Lives*. 9 vols.
Mag's Diversions. 4 vols.*
Swallows *On Emigration*. 2 vols.
Shelley's *Oysters.*
The Pleasures of Boredom. A Poem.
Drowsy's *Recollections of Nothing*. 3 vols.
Treatise on the Tape Worm. By Tim Bobbin.
The Wisdom of our Ancestors. Vol. I *Ignorance*, Vol. II *Superstition*,
 Vol. III *The Block,* Vol. IV *The Stake,* Vol. V *The Rack,* Vol. VI *Dirt,*
 Vol. VII *Disease.*

---

* *Mag's Diversions* was one of the working titles for *David Copperfield* (see also p.78).

BOOKS SET *in our* SOLAR SYSTEM

'Once it gets off the ground into space,' wrote J. G. Ballard, 'all science fiction is fantasy.' Starting with Lucian of Samosata in the second century AD, many writers have dreamed up tales set elsewhere in our solar system.

THE SUN *Sundiver* by David Brin • *The Flames* by Olaf Stapledon

MERCURY *The World of Mercury* by the Chevalier de Béthune
The Immortals of Mercury by Clark Ashton Smith

VENUS *The Oceans of Venus* by Isaac Asimov • *Pirates of Venus* by Edgar Rice Burroughs • *Voyage to Venus* by Achille Eyraud • *Perelandra* by C. S. Lewis • *A Trip to Venus* by John Munro

THE MOON *The Consolidator* by Daniel Defoe • *The Man in the Moone* by Francis Godwin • *The Moon is a Harsh Mistress* by Robert A. Heinlein
The Dream by Johannes Kepler • *The True History* by Lucian of Samosata
The Lunatic Republic by Compton Mackenzie • *The Hopkins Manuscript* by R. C. Sherriff • *From the Earth to the Moon* by Jules Verne • *The First Men in the Moon* by H. G. Wells

MARS *The Martian Chronicles* by Ray Bradbury • *A Princess of Mars* by Edgar Rice Burroughs • *Martian Time-Slip* by Philip K. Dick • *The Martian* by George du Maurier • *Red Planet* by Robert A. Heinlein • *Out of the Silent Planet* by C. S. Lewis • *The Man Who Fell to Earth* by Walter Tevis*
The Martian by Andy Weir • *The War of the Worlds* by H. G. Wells

JUPITER *A Journey in Other Worlds* by John Jacob Astor IV
The Perfect World by Ella Scrymsour

SATURN *2001: A Space Odyssey* by Arthur C. Clarke† • *Micromégas* by Voltaire • *The Sirens of Titan* by Kurt Vonnegut

URANUS 'The Planet of Doubt' by Stanley G. Weinbaum • *Floating Worlds* by Cecelia Holland

NEPTUNE *Last and First Men* by Olaf Stapledon • *Triton* by Samuel R. Delaney

PLUTO *First Lensman* by E. E. Smith • *The Secret of the Ninth Planet* by Donald A. Wollheim

---

* In Tevis's novel, the man – played by David Bowie in Nicholas Roeg's film adaptation – comes from the planet Anthea, which seems to be the planet we call Mars.

† In Clarke's novel, the titular 'odyssey' is a mission to Iapetus, the third moon of Saturn; in Stanley Kubrick's film version, the mission is to Jupiter.

The BIGGEST WORDS YOU EVER HEARD

'I am a bear of very little brain,' says Winnie-the-Pooh, 'and long words bother me.' One of the longest words in French is *hippopotomonstrosesquippedaliophobie* (thirty-six letters), meaning 'a fear of long words', and the longest non-technical word in English is *floccinaucinihilipilification* (twenty-nine letters), meaning 'the habit of describing something as worthless'. The longest word on record is a 183-letter recipe in *The Assemblywomen* by Aristophanes. Here are a few other sesquipedalianisms:

dziewięćsetdziewięćdziesiątdziewięćmiliardówdziewięćsetdziewięćdziesiątdziewięćmilionówdziewięćsetdziewięćdziesiątdziewięćtysięcydziewięćsetdziewięćdziesięciodziewięcioletniego – '999,999,999,999 years old', (Polish, 176 letters)

spårvagnsaktiebolagsskensmutsskjutarefackföreningspersonalbeklädnadsmagasinsförrådsförvaltarens – 'belonging to the manager of the depot for supplying uniforms to the personnel of the track cleaners' union of the tramway company' (Swedish, ninety-five letters)

Donaudampfschiffahrtselektrizitätenhauptbetriebswerkbauunterbeamtengesellschaft – 'association for the subordinate officials of the main maintenance building of the Danube Steam Ship Electrical Services Company' (German, seventy-nine letters)

vastatykistömaalinosoitustutkakalustojärjestelmäinsinöörierikoisupseeri – 'counter-artillery targeting radar systems engineer specialist officer' (Finnish, seventy-one letters)

miinibaashkiminasiganibiitoosijiganibadagwiingweshiganibakwezhigan – 'blueberry pie' (Ojibwe, sixty-six letters)*

vaðlaheiðarvegavinnuverkfærageymsluskúraútidyralyklakippuhringur – 'a key ring for the outdoor key of the road workers' shed on a moor called Vaðlaheiði' (Icelandic, sixty-four letters)

speciallægepraksisplanlægningsstabiliseringsperiode – 'a period of stabilizing the organization of a specialist doctor's practice' (Danish, fifty-one letters)

sünnipäevanädalalõpupeopärastlõunaväsimatus – 'exhaustion at a birthday-week graduation party' (Estonian, forty-three letters)

---

* The Ojibwe people live in southern Canada (Ontario and Manitoba) and the northern USA (Minnesota and North Dakota); today Ojibwe is the native language for around 50,000 people.

The GOLDEN NOTEBOOK

Doris Lessing's novel alternates sections of *Free Women*, a novel by the fictional novelist Anna Wulf, with extracts from Wulf's colour-coded notebooks, which she uses to record different aspects of her life.

Black Notebook (*Southern Rhodesia*) · Red Notebook (*Communism*)
Yellow Notebook (*a love affair*) · Blue Notebook (*memories and dreams*)

SHĪSHÌ SHÍ SHĪ SHǏ

The Chinese poet Yuen Ren Chao wrote the ninety-five-character poem 'Shīshì shí shī shǐ' ('Lion-Eating Poet in the Stone Den') to demonstrate the number of homophones in spoken Mandarin. The poem is intelligible when written in Chinese characters, but becomes incomprehensible when read aloud, because it uses only four tonal sounds.*

Shíshì shīshì Shī Shì, shì shī, shì shí shí shī.

Shì Shì shíshí shì shì shì shī.

Shí shí, shì shí shī shì shì.

Shì shí, shì Shī Shì shì shì.

Shì Shì shì shì shí shī, shì shǐ shì, shì shǐ shí shī shìshì.

Shì shí shì shí shī shī, shì shíshì.

Shíshì shī, Shì shǐ shì shì shì shíshì.

Shíshì shì, Shì shǐ shì shì shí shì shí shī shī.

Shí shí, shì shí shì shí shī shī, shí shí shí shī shī.

Shì shì shì shì.

* The poem translates as follows: 'In a stone den was a poet called Shi, who was a lion addict, and had resolved to eat ten lions. / He often went to the market to look for lions. / At ten o'clock, ten lions had just arrived at the market. / At the same time, Shi had just arrived at the market. / He saw those ten lions, and using his trusty arrows, killed the ten lions. / He brought the corpses of the ten lions to the stone den. / The stone den was damp. He asked his servants to clean it. / Once the stone den was dry, he tried to eat those ten lions. / When he ate, he realized that the ten lions were in fact ten stone lion corpses. / Try to explain this matter.'

THE FIRST VOYAGE

THE SECOND VOYAGE

THE THIRD VOYAGE

THE FOURTH VOYAGE

The TRAVELS of GULLIVER

In *Gulliver's Travels* by Jonathan Swift, the ship's surgeon Lemuel Gulliver describes his final four voyages 'into several remote nations of the world', between each of which he returns to his wife and children in Rotherhithe, London. 'I could perhaps like others have astonished thee with strange improbable Tales,' he reassures readers at the end of his book; 'but I rather chose to relate plain Matter of Fact, in the simplest Manner and Style.'

THE FIRST VOYAGE (*4 May 1699–13 April 1702*)

Lilliput, an island north-west of Van Diemen's Land (Tasmania)
  'the common Size of the Natives is somewhat under six Inches high'

Blefuscu, an island north-east of Lilliput
  'the other great Empire of the Universe'

THE SECOND VOYAGE (*20 June 1702–3 June 1706*)

Brobdingnag, a peninsula off north-west America
  'one of the Inhabitants [...] appeared as tall as an ordinary Spire-steeple'

THE THIRD VOYAGE (*5 August 1706–20 April 1710*)

Laputa, the flying island, above Balnibarbi
  'the most delicious spot of Ground in the World'

Balnibarbi, an island north-west of Luggnagg
  'subject to the Monarch of the *Flying Island*'

Glubbdubdrib, a small island, south-west of Balnibarbi
  'the Island of *Sorcerers* or *Magicians*'

Luggnagg, an island south-east of Japan
  'this Breed of *Struldbruggs* was peculiar to their Country'

Japan, an island east of China
  'my Stay in *Japan* was [...] short'

THE FOURTH VOYAGE (*7 September 1710–5 December 1715*)

The Land of the Houyhnhnms, an island in the south Indian Ocean,
      somewhere off south-west Australia
  'the Word *Houyhnhnm*, in their Tongue, signifies a *Horse*, and in
  its Etymology, *the Perfection of Nature*'

The WARBURG LIBRARY

The art historian Aby Warburg compiled his vast library of 60,000 books and 25,000 photographs – the *Kulturwissenschaftliche Bibliothek Warburg* – in Hamburg, Germany. After his death in 1929, it moved to the UK and was eventually incorporated into the University of London. Today the cross-disciplinary Warburg Institute in Bloomsbury specializes in the history of art, science, magic and religion, and its library maintains Warburg's idiosyncratic organizational principles. Warburg believed in the 'good neighbourhood of books', and the arrangement of the library is designed to encourage serendipitous discoveries and open unexpected avenues of research. The floors are arranged thematically as follows:

4th floor	ACTION	Society, Culture, History, Magic and Science
3rd floor	ORIENTATION	Western and Eastern Religions, Philosophy
2nd floor	WORD	Language and Literature
1st floor	IMAGE	Art History
Ground floor	READING ROOM	Reference Works

The HUNTERS of the SNARK

In his nonsense poem *The Hunting of the Snark*, Lewis Carroll described an eccentric expedition in quest of a Snark, a lazy feathered creature with a poor sense of humour, who adores bathing machines and tastes good with greens. The ten-strong crew arrive on a distant shore and set about pursuing the Snark with thimbles and care, forks and hope, smiles and soap.

Bellman • Boots • Bonnet-maker • Barrister • Broker • Billiard-marker
Banker • Beaver • Baker* • Butcher

---

* The mysterious Baker has an uncle who warns him about Snarks that are Boojums. Alas, when the Baker discovers a Snark, it is a Boojum, and he softly and silently vanishes away.

The POETS LAUREATE

The office of Poet Laureate of the United Kingdom is an honorary position appointed by the monarch. Although Ben Jonson was granted a royal pension by King James VI and I, the first official laureate was John Dryden, appointed by King Charles II. Dryden's salary was £200 a year and a tierce of canary wine; today the salary is £5,750 and a butt of sherry. The laureateship has been refused by, among others, Thomas Gray in 1757, Walter Scott in 1813 and Philip Larkin in 1984. Samuel Rogers, who refused the honour in 1850, lent the same tailcoat and breeches to Wordsworth and Tennyson for their official investitures at the palace.

John Dryden	1668–1688
Thomas Shadwell	1689–1692
Nahum Tate	1692–1715
Nicholas Rowe	1715–1718
Laurence Eusden	1718–1730
Colley Cibber	1730–1757
William Whitehead	1757–1785
Thomas Warton	1785–1790
Henry James Pye*	1790–1813
Robert Southey	1813–1843
William Wordsworth	1843–1850
Alfred, Lord Tennyson	1850–1892†
Alfred Austin	1896–1913
Robert Bridges	1913–1930
John Masefield	1930–1967
Cecil Day-Lewis	1968–1972
John Betjeman	1972–1984
Ted Hughes	1984–1998
Andrew Motion	1999–2009
Carol Ann Duffy	2009–2019
Simon Armitage	2019–

* Henry Pye was a notoriously dreadful poet. His first effort for George III was full of allusions to 'feathered songsters' and so bad that his contemporary George Stevens quipped: 'When the Pye was opened, the birds began to sing; was not that a dainty dish to set before a king?'

† Tennyson has had the longest tenure as laureate, forty-two years; after his death, there was a four-year break before a successor was appointed. The post used to be for life, but since Sir Andrew Motion's appointment in 1999 it has lasted ten years.

Some AUTHORS who DIED YOUNG

In 2004, scientists at California State University, San Bernardino, analysed 1,987 dead authors and found that poets died 'significantly younger' than novelists, playwrights and other writers. These authors all died young:

aged seventeen	Thomas Chatterton	1752–1770
aged twenty	Raymond Radiguet	1903–1923
aged twenty-one	Toru Dutt*	1856–1877
aged twenty-three	Georg Büchner	1813–1837
aged twenty-four	Keith Douglas	1920–1944
	Comte de Lautréamont	1846–1870
aged twenty-five	Andrés Caicedo	1951–1977
	John Keats	1795–1821
	Wilfred Owen	1893–1918
aged twenty-six	Mikhail Lermontov	1814–1841
aged twenty-seven	Alain-Fournier	1886–1914
	Rupert Brooke	1887–1915
	Georg Trakl	1887–1914
aged twenty-eight	Tadeusz Borowski	1922–1951
	Stephen Crane	1871–1900
	Novalis	1772–1801
aged twenty-nine	Anne Brontë	1820–1849
	Richard Fariña†	1937–1966
	Christopher Marlowe	1564–1593
	Ippolito Nievo	1831–1861
	Percy Bysshe Shelley	1792–1822
aged thirty	W. N. P. Barbellion	1889–1919
	Emily Brontë	1818–1848
	Catullus	c.84–c.54 BC
	Sylvia Plath	1932–1963

* Toru Dutt was a Bengali prodigy from Calcutta, who learned Milton's *Paradise Lost* by heart, translated Sanskrit ballads into English and wrote two novels, one in English and one in French. She is one of only four women on this list: confirmation, perhaps, that in a literary world dominated by men, women have historically taken longer to establish their reputations.

† Richard Fariña's only novel, *Been Down So Long It Looks Like Up to Me*, became a cult bestseller of the 1960s. It's a picaresque adventure involving mescaline, eastern religion, a monkey demon and feta cheese. Thomas Pynchon called it 'hilarious, chilling, sexy, profound, maniacal, beautiful and outrageous'. Fariña died in a motorcycle accident two days after publication.

The **DEWEY DECIMAL SYSTEM**

Originally conceived in 1876 by Melvil Dewey, the chief librarian at Columbia University in New York, the Dewey Decimal Classification is used today in more than 200,000 libraries around the world. Three-digit numbers are given to main classes – 823, for example, is 'English fiction' – and subsequent digits may be assigned for more detailed subdivisions: 823.01 means 'short stories in English'. The system is updated quarterly.

000–099	General works
100–199	Philosophy and Psychology
200–299	Religion
300–399	Social sciences
400–499	Languages
500–599	Science
600–699	Technology
700–799	Arts and Recreation
800 899	Literature
900–999	History and Geography

INTERROGATIVE TITLES

Some titles ask questions. Here are some answers.

Who's Afraid of Virginia Woolf?	by	Edward Albee	Martha
N or M?	by	Agatha Christie	N and M
Do Androids Dream of Electric Sheep?	by	Philip K. Dick	no
May We Borrow Your Husband?	by	Graham Greene	yes
Is God Happy?	by	Leszek Kołakowski	no
What Is to Be Done?	by	Vladimir Lenin	unite
If Not Now, When?	by	Primo Levi	now
They Shoot Horses, Don't They?	by	Horace McCoy	yes
How Much Land Does a Man Need?	by	Leo Tolstoy	six feet
Can You Forgive Her?	by	Anthony Trollope	yes

The VERY HUNGRY CATERPILLAR

Having eaten through an apple, two pears, three plums, four strawberries and five oranges in the week, the very hungry caterpillar in Eric Carle's eponymously titled children's book is still hungry. On Saturday, he eats:

one piece of chocolate cake,
one ice-cream cone,
one pickle,
one slice of swiss cheese,
one slice of salami,
one lollipop,
one piece of cherry pie,
one sausage,
one cupcake, and
one slice of watermelon.

That night he had a stomachache!

The HARLEM RENAISSANCE

In the 1920s, an explosion of Black cultural and intellectual activity took place in Harlem, New York: the 'New Negro' movement sought to express every aspect of the Black cultural and political experience in America. In his preface to *The Book of American Negro Poetry*, a landmark publication in 1922, the poet James Weldon Johnson pointed out that Black literature and music were 'the only things artistic that have yet sprung from American soil and been universally acknowledged as distinctive American products'. Writers associated with the Harlem Renaissance include:

Arna Bontemps • Countee Cullen • Jessie Fauset • Rudolph Fisher
Langston Hughes • Zora Neale Hurston* • Nella Larsen • Alain Locke
Claude McKay • Willis Richardson • Anne Spencer • Wallace Thurman
Jean Toomer • Eric D. Walrond

* Hurston was a trained anthropologist. She is best remembered for her novel *Their Eyes Were Watching God*, about a Black woman searching for meaning and love in 1930s Florida.

ISHMAEL'S WHALES

In *Moby-Dick* by Herman Melville, the narrator – Ishmael – lists 'all the Leviathans of note' in a chapter called 'Cetology'. He organizes the whales as if they were in a library, under different book sizes (see p.54).

THE DUODECIMO WHALES

The Huzza Porpoise
'The common porpoise found almost all over the globe.'

The Algerine Porpoise
'A pirate. Very savage.'

The Mealy-mouthed Porpoise
'A neat and gentleman-like figure.'

THE OCTAVO WHALES

The Grampus
'[His] loud sonorous breathing, or rather blowing, has furnished a proverb to landsmen.'*

The Black Fish
'He carries an everlasting Mephistophelean grin on his face.'

The Narwhale
'Some sixteen feet in length, while its horn averages five feet.'

The Killer
'About the bigness of a grampus. He is very savage.'

The Thrasher
'Famous for his tail, which he uses for a ferule in thrashing his foes.'

THE FOLIO WHALES

The Sperm Whale
'The largest inhabitant of the globe; the most formidable of all whales to encounter; the most majestic in aspect.'

The Right Whale
'Most venerable of the leviathans, being the one first regularly hunted.'

The Fin-Back
'Commonly the whale whose distant jet is so often descried by passengers crossing the Atlantic.'

The Hump Back
'He has a great pack on him like a peddler; or you might call him the Elephant and Castle whale.'

The Razor Back
'Of a retiring nature, he eludes both hunters and philosophers.'

The Sulphur Bottom
'Another retiring gentleman, with a brimstone belly, doubtless got by scraping along the Tartarian tiles in some of his profounder divings.'

* 'To puff like a grampus' – first recorded in 1837, in *The Pickwick Papers* by Charles Dickens.

The ELVISH SCRIPTS

J. R. R. Tolkien constructed fictional languages and scripts throughout his life. He called the habit *glossopoeia* and spoke about it in a 1931 lecture entitled 'A Secret Vice'. 'The invention of languages is the foundation,' he wrote. 'The "stories" were made rather to provide a world for the languages than the reverse.' Tolkien created two fully developed Elvish languages, Quenya and Sindarin, and fragments of several others. These could be written in the Latin alphabet or in a range of scripts, also invented by Tolkien, who had been a talented calligrapher since childhood. He called his principal Elvish scripts the Sarati, the Tengwar and the Cirth.

THE SARATI

The Sarati, or 'the Tengwar of Rúmil', was the first script Tolkien developed. It is written vertically like Ogham (see p.94). In his fictional world, the Sarati was an ancient script developed among a group of Elves called the Noldor, when they were living in Valinor to the west of Middle-earth. The Elves were ambidextrous, so vertical lines of Sarati can be written right-to-left or left-to-right. Tolkien first wrote in Sarati in his diary in 1919.

THE TENGWAR

When some of the Noldor returned to Middle-Earth, they brought with them a refinement of Sarati known as 'Tengwar', or 'the Tengwar of Fëanor'. This is the Elvish script that features in *The Lord of the Rings*.

Tolkien wrote this text himself for *The Fellowship of the Ring*. It appears in letters of fire on the ring that Frodo Baggins inherits from his cousin Bilbo, the protagonist of *The Hobbit*, who found it in the Goblin caves, near Gollum's lair. The wizard Gandalf (see p.33) translates the text as follows:

One Ring to rule them all, One Ring to find them,
One Ring to bring them all and in the darkness bind them.

The Cirth were developed independently by another group of Elves, the Sindar of Beleriand. Cirth are more angular and were later adapted by Men and Dwarves to transcribe their languages. Tolkien wrote out the Cirth for an appendix – 'Writing and Spelling' – at the end of *The Lord of the Rings*. The letters are based on ancient Germanic rune alphabets.

If you wish to delve further into Elvish languages and scripts, you might consider attending the next *Omentielva*, the International Conference on J. R. R. Tolkien's Invented Languages. These conferences have been held biennially since 2005, in different cities, including Stockholm, Antwerp, Valencia and Reykjavik. The programme features a series of academic lectures as well as Quenya poetry competitions, workshops on 'practical Elvish', and seminars on bringing Elvish scripts and languages into the digital age. Full details on the website: omentielva.com.

Some LITERARY PUBS

In 1946, George Orwell wrote the essay 'The Moon Under Water', in which he fantasized about his ideal pub, specifying 'uncompromisingly Victorian' fittings, 'a good fire burning' and the requirement that it is 'always quiet enough to talk'. He came up with the pub's name, and the J D Wetherspoon chain has since called several of its pubs 'The Moon Under Water'. Here are some public houses that appear in works of fiction:

The Admiral Benbow	*Treasure Island*	Robert Louis Stevenson
The Angler's Rest	The *Mr Mulliner* series	P. G. Wodehouse
The Black Cross	*London Fields*	Martin Amis
The Boar's Head	*Henry IV, Parts 1 & 2*	William Shakespeare
The Chatsubo	*Neuromancer*	William Gibson*
The Coach and Horses	*Last Orders*	Graham Swift
The Cow and Hedge	*The Diary of a Nobody*	George & Weedon Grossmith
Davy Byrne's	*Ulysses*	James Joyce
The Downy Pelican	*Poet's Pub*	Eric Linklater
The Dragon of Wantley	*The Barchester Chronicles*	Anthony Trollope
The Harbinger	*The Ballad of Peckham Rye*	Muriel Spark
The Horse and Groom	*The Hitch Hiker's Guide to the Galaxy*	Douglas Adams
The Leaky Cauldron	The *Harry Potter* series	J. K. Rowling
The Midnight Bell	*Twenty Thousand Streets Under the Sky*	Patrick Hamilton
The Prancing Pony	*The Lord of the Rings*	J. R. R. Tolkien
The Sailor's Arms	*Under Milk Wood*	Dylan Thomas
The Six Jolly Fellowship Porters	*Our Mutual Friend*	Charles Dickens
The Tabard	*The Canterbury Tales*	Geoffrey Chaucer
The Three Pigeons	*She Stoops to Conquer*	Oliver Goldsmith

* *Neuromancer* is the only novel to have won the Hugo Award, the Nebula Award and the Philip K. Dick Award, the three most prestigious science fiction prizes. It is a 'cyberpunk' novel, set in a dystopian Japanese underworld, where lowlife crooks collaborate with hi-tech cyborgs.

The FOUR ZOAS

The poet William Blake constructed a complex personal mythology around his concept of the four archetypal aspects of human nature: the 'Zoas'.

Tharmas (the body) • *Urizen* (reason)
Luvah (emotions) • *Urthona* (the imagination)

The HEAVENLY EMPORIUM

In a 1942 essay, Jorge Luis Borges described a fictional Chinese encyclopaedia, the *Heavenly Emporium of Benevolent Knowledge*, which contains an unusual taxonomy of the animal kingdom. Michel Foucault was particularly fascinated by this list, which inspired him to write his book *The Order of Things*. In Foucault's words, Borges's list 'shattered' the way we think, 'breaking up all the ordered surfaces and all the planes with which we are accustomed to tame the wild profusion of existing things'.

It is written that animals are divided into
- (a) those that belong to the emperor;
- (b) embalmed ones;
- (c) those that are trained;
- (d) suckling pigs;
- (e) mermaids;
- (f) fabulous ones;
- (g) stray dogs;
- (h) those that are included in this classification;*
- (i) those that tremble as if they were mad;
- (j) innumerable ones;
- (k) those drawn with a very fine camel's-hair brush;
- (l) et cetera;
- (m) those that have just broken the flower vase;
- (n) those that at a distance resemble flies.

---

* 'The thing that makes the list really disquieting,' wrote Umberto Eco, 'is that, among the elements it classifies, it also includes those already classified. [...] With Borges's classification the poetics of the list reaches the acme of heresy and blasphemes all preconstituted logical order.'

BLYTON'S CHILDREN

Enid Blyton wrote several long-running series of books about different groups of children. She claimed to write without revision: 'I am [...] able to write a story and read it for the first time, at one and the same moment.'

The Famous Five	Julian, Dick, George, Anne and Timmy the dog
The Secret Seven	Peter, Janet, Pam, Barbara, Jack, Colin and George
The Adventurous Four	Jill, Mary, Tom and Andy
The Five Find-Outers	Fatty, Larry, Pip, Daisy and Bets
The Adventure Series	Philip, Jack, Dinah and Lucy-Ann

LETTERS *for* TITLES

'Letters for titles,' muses Stephen Dedalus in James Joyce's *Ulysses*. 'Have you read his F? O yes, but I prefer Q. Yes, but W is wonderful. O yes, W.' *F*, *Q* and *W* have all since been written, in fact most of the alphabet has been covered, although no one has yet published a book called *R*.

a	Andy Warhol	*N*	Arthur Machen
B	Sarah Kay	*O*	anonymous
C	Tom McCarthy		(possibly Mark Salter)
D	Michel Faber	*P*	Andrew Lewis Conn
e	Matthew Beaumont	*Q*	Luther Blissett*
F	Daniel Kehlmann	*S.*	John Updike
G.	John Berger	*t*	Victor Pelevin
H	Philippe Sollers	*U*	Markku Into
I.	Stephen Dixon	*V.*	Thomas Pynchon
J	Howard Jacobson	*W*	Georges Perec
K.	Roberto Calasso	*X*	Sue Grafton (see p.18)
L	Erlend Loe	*Y*	Marjorie Celona
M	John Sack	*Z*	Therese Anne Fowler

* The name Luther Blissett has been used by many different artists, activists and hoaxers since 1994. The real Luther Blissett is a football player who played for England in the 1980s. In the case of *Q*, the pen name refers to four Italian authors who live in Bologna and wrote the novel together: Roberto Bui, Giovanni Cattabriga, Federico Guglielmi and Luca Di Meo.

The THOUSAND SHIPS

When Paris elopes with Helen, the wife of Menelaus, the Greeks launch 'a thousand ships' to cross the Aegean and lay siege to Troy. Led by Menelaus' older brother Agamemnon (see p.141), every Greek kingdom contributes a contingent: 1,186 in total. They are listed in Book 2 of Homer's *Iliad*.

100	Mycenaean ships, led by Agamemnon*
90	Pylian ships, from Messenia, led by Nestor*
80	Argives, led by Diomedes,* Sthenelus & Euryalus
	Cretans, led by Idomeneus* & Meriones
60	Arcadians, led by Agapenor
	Lacedaemonians, from Sparta, led by Menelaus*
50	Athenians, led by Menestheus
	Boeotians, led by Peneleus, Leitus, Arcesilaus, Prothoenor & Clonius
	Pelasgians, Myrmidons, Hellenes & Achaeans led by Achilles*
40	Abantes, from Euboea, led by Elephenor
	Aetolians, led by Thoas
	Dolichians, led by Meges
	Epeians, led by Amphimachus, Thalpius, Diores & Polyxenus
	Lapiths, from Peneus, led by Polypoetes & Leonteus
	Locrians, led by Ajax the Lesser*
	Magnesians, led by Prothous
	Phoceans, led by Schedius & Epistrophus
	Ormenians, led by Eurypylus
	Phylacians, from Phthiotis, led by Protesilaus, then Podarces
30	Minyans, from Aspledon, led by Ascalaphus & Ialmenus
	Nisyrians, led by Pheidippus & Antiphus
	Oechalians, from Peneius, led by Podalirius & Machaon
22	Enienes, from Cyphus, led by Guncus
12	Cephallenians, led by Odysseus*
	Salamineans, led by Ajax the Great*
11	Thessalians, from Pherae and Iolcus, led by Eumelus
9	Rhodians, led by Tlepolemus
7	Meliboeans, from Methone & Thaumacia, led by Philoctetes, then Medon
3	Symians, led by Nireus

* These are the major Greek characters in *The Iliad*. The godlike Achilles is the greatest Greek warrior, whose only vulnerability is his heel; the cunning Odysseus becomes the central character in Homer's *Odyssey*; the wise Nestor is the eldest Greek leader; the enormous Ajax the Great is immensely strong; the young Diomedes is skilful and strategic; Ajax the Lesser is brave; and Idomeneus is one of Agamemnon's most trusted advisors.

The KNIGHTS *of the* ROUND TABLE

In the legends of King Arthur, he gathers a fellowship of courtly knights who sit as equals around a circular table. The identity and number of the knights varies in different versions of the story, but the following are among the most prominent in the English, Welsh and French traditions:

Sir Agravain · *Sir* Bedivere · *Sir* Bors · *Sir* Brunor · *Sir* Constantine
Sir Dagonet · *Sir* Ector · *Sir* Gaheris · *Sir* Galahad · *Sir* Gareth
Sir Gawain · *Sir* Geraint · *Sir* Lamorak · *Sir* Lancelot · *Sir* Lionel
Sir Lucan · *Sir* Kay · *Sir* Mordred · *Sir* Palomedes · *Sir* Pelleas
Sir Perceval · *Sir* Safir · *Sir* Tristram · *Sir* Ywain

LITERARY SYNDROMES

In 1910, Freud named his notorious Oedipus complex – a son's desire for his mother and jealousy of his father – after Oedipus in Sophocles' tragedy, and Jung's Electra complex is named after the daughter of Agamemnon (see p.141). Other maladies named after fictional characters include:

ALICE IN WONDERLAND SYNDROME *where objects and body parts appear too large or too small* ¶ BOVARISM *a tendency towards escapist daydreaming* ¶ DORIAN GRAY SYNDROME *a preoccupation with maintaining one's physical attractiveness* ¶ LADY WINDERMERE SYNDROME *a pulmonary infection associated with stifled coughs* ¶ HUCKLEBERRY FINN SYNDROME *a tendency to flee from commitments* ¶ MUNCHAUSEN SYNDROME *the self-infliction of symptoms to maintain the illusion of illness* ¶ OTHELLO SYNDROME *a delusional belief in one's partner's infidelity* ¶ PETER PAN SYNDROME *a refusal to grow up and accept responsibilities* ¶ PICKWICKIAN SYNDROME *a tendency for obese people to fall asleep during the day** ¶ RIP VAN WINKLE SYNDROME *intermittent episodes of hypersomnolence*

---

* This syndrome is named after Joe 'the fat boy', who repeatedly falls asleep in *The Pickwick Papers* by Charles Dickens. Also known as 'obesity hypoventilation syndrome', it's a condition in which obesity leads to low oxygen levels at night and sleepiness during the day.

Some POETIC TITLES

Antic Hay by Aldous Huxley
'My men, like satyrs grazing on the lawns, / Shall with their goat-feet dance the antic hay.' (*Edward II* by Christopher Marlowe)

As I Lay Dying by William Faulkner
'As I lay dying, the woman with the dog's eyes would not close my eyes as I descended into Hades.' (*The Odyssey* by Homer)

Dance Dance Dance by Haruki Murakami
'Dance till the stars come down from the rafters; / Dance, dance, dance till you drop.' ('Death's Echo' by W. H. Auden)

Endless Night by Agatha Christie
'Some are Born to sweet delight / Some are Born to Endless Night.' ('Auguries of Innocence' by William Blake)

Far From the Madding Crowd by Thomas Hardy
'Far from the madding crowd's ignoble strife, / Their sober wishes never learn'd to stray.' ('Elegy Written in a Country Churchyard' by Thomas Gray)

A Handful of Dust by Evelyn Waugh
'I will show you fear in a handful of dust.' (*The Waste Land* by T. S. Eliot)

No Highway by Nevil Shute
'When you find / No highway more, no track, all being blind / The way to go shall glimmer in the mind.' ('The Ending' by John Masefield)

Of Mice and Men by John Steinbeck
'The best-laid schemes o' Mice an' Men / Gang aft agley.' ('To a Mouse' by Robert Burns)

O Pioneers! by Willa Cather
'Plain I see you Western youths, see you tramping with the foremost, / Pioneers! O pioneers!' (*Leaves of Grass* by Walt Whitman)

Things Fall Apart by Chinua Achebe
'Things fall apart; the centre cannot hold; / Mere anarchy is loosed upon the world.' ('The Second Coming' by W. B. Yeats)

A Thousand Splendid Suns by Khaled Hosseini
'One could not count the moons that shimmer on her roofs / And the thousand splendid suns that hide behind her walls.' ('Kabul' by Saib Tabrizi)

POINTS *d'*INTONATION

In his 1966 book, *Plumons l'oiseau* ('Let's pluck the bird'), the novelist Hervé Bazin proposed a new 'phonemic orthography' for the French language, including six punctuation marks, designed to indicate specific intonation.

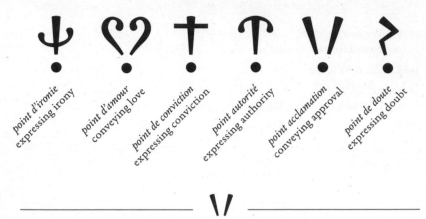

point d'ironie expressing irony • point d'amour conveying love • point de conviction expressing conviction • point autorité expressing authority • point acclamation conveying approval • point de doute expressing doubt

The WOOD *of* SUICIDES

In the seventh circle of Dante's *Inferno*, Dante and Virgil pass through the 'Wood of Suicides', where thorny trees contain the souls of those who have taken their own lives. The following writers cut their lives short:

Ryunosuke Akutagawa • John Berryman • Tadeusz Borowski
Paul Celan • Thomas Chatterton • Hart Crane • Tove Ditlevsen
Charlotte Perkins Gilman • Ernest Hemingway • B. S. Johnson
Yasunari Kawabata • Heinrich von Kleist • Arthur Koestler
Primo Levi • Lucretius • Yukio Mishima* • Cesare Pavese • Petronius
Sylvia Plath • Jan Potocki† • Seneca • Anne Sexton‡ • Hunter S.
Thompson • John Kennedy Toole • Virginia Woolf • Stefan Zweig

---

* Mishima attempted to incite an insurrection at a military base near Tokyo in 1970. After a rousing speech from a balcony, which was greeted by jeers, he shouted 'Long live the Emperor!' before stepping inside and performing *seppuku*, ritual disembowelment.
† The Polish nobleman Count Potocki, believing himself to be a werewolf, took his own life with a silver bullet modelled from the knob of his favourite sugar-bowl.
‡ The poet Anne Sexton contemplated suicide frequently, comparing herself to 'a moth sucking an electric bulb'.

The ODDEST TITLE of the YEAR

The Diagram Prize was conceived in 1978 by the Diagram Group, a design company, and since then it has been awarded annually by the *Bookseller* magazine. The year's oddest book title is decided by a public vote and a bottle of claret awarded to the nominator. Here is a selection of winners:

1978	*Proceedings of the Second International Workshop on Nude Mice**	various
1984	*The Book of Marmalade: Its Antecedents, Its History, and Its Role in the World Today*	Anne Wilson
1986	*Oral Sadism and the Vegetarian Personality*	Glenn C. Ellenbogen
1988	*Versailles: The View from Sweden*	Elaine Dee & Guy Walton
1992	*How to Avoid Huge Ships*	John W. Trimmer
1994	*Highlights in the History of Concrete*	C. C. Stanley
1996	*Greek Rural Postmen and Their Cancellation Numbers**	Derek Willan
2002	*Living with Crazy Buttocks*	Kaz Cooke
2003	*The Big Book of Lesbian Horse Stories*	Alisa Surkis & Monica Nolan
2006	*The Stray Shopping Carts of Eastern North America: A Guide to Field Identification*	Julian Montague
2009	*Crocheting Adventures with Hyperbolic Planes*	Daina Taimina
2010	*Managing a Dental Practice: The Genghis Khan Way*	Michael R. Young
2012	*Goblinproofing One's Chicken Coop*	Reginald Bakeley
2013	*How to Poo on a Date*	Mats & Enzo
2015	*Too Naked for the Nazis*	Alan Stafford
2018	*The Joy of Water Boiling*	Thomas Götz von Aust
2019	*The Dirt Hole and Its Variations*	Charles L. Dobbins
2020	*A Dog Pissing at the Edge of a Path: Animal Metaphors in an Eastern Indonesian Society*	Gregory Forth
2021	*Is Superman Circumcised?†*	Roy Schwartz

* These two titles won the 'Diagram of Diagrams' anniversary awards in 1993 and 2008.
† Probably. For answers to more interrogative titles see p.111.

Johannes Gutenberg introduced the movable-type printing press to Europe in 1450. His innovation was to arrange metal 'type' – cast letters in relief – within a frame: he covered their surface in ink and pressed them on to paper to print a page. He was then able to rearrange the type within the frame to create more pages. Movable type meant the 'typeface' of the letters remained consistent throughout an entire book. Over the years, printers and designers have experimented with different styles. This book, for example, is set in Garalda, a French-style serif typeface.

BLACKLETTER, OR GOTHIC

Gutenberg's preferred type was 'blackletter', which imitated the medieval handwritten manuscripts of western Europe. This style was used widely for many centuries, especially for texts printed in Denmark, Sweden and Germany. Adolf Hitler discontinued the use of blackletter in Germany in 1941; it is still common in newspaper mastheads around the world.

Textura	**Rotunda**	**Schwabacher**	**Fraktur**
The earliest, most calligraphic form	A less angular, Italian variation	Used in early German printing	Used from the sixteenth century
Old English	*Rotunda*	*Schwabacher*	*Fraktur*

SERIF, OR ROMAN

In 1465, Venetian printers began developing a new style of typeface, based on Roman square capitals and Renaissance calligraphy with 'serifs', the small ornamental strokes that embellish a letter. These typefaces could be presented upright or, from 1500, in a cursive variation known as 'italic' (because it originated in Italy), designed to approximate handwriting.

Venetian	**French**	**Dutch**	**Transitional**
Round and even with short serifs	Finely proportioned	A denser, more solid variation	Also known as 'baroque'
Bembo	*Garamond*	*Ehrhardt*	*Baskerville*

Modern	**Slab serif**	**Clarendon**	**Glyphic**
Narrow serifs, contrasting thick and thin lines	A thick, geometric design, designed for display purposes	A bold, sturdy structure with curved slab serifs	Triangular serifs with tapering stroke ends
Ii	**Jj**	**Kk**	**Ll**
Bodoni	*Rockwell*	*Clarendon*	*Albertus*

SANS-SERIF, OR EGYPTIAN*

Towards the end of the eighteenth century, typefaces without serifs began to appear, pioneered initially by the British architect John Soane on his hand-drawn designs, inspired perhaps by Etruscan inscriptions. They became popular for signage because they were easily legible at a distance. Later, in the early twentieth century, artists began to produce clean sans-serif typefaces that complemented the new age of modernism.

Grotesque[†]	**Neo-grotesque**	**Geometric**	**Humanist**
The earliest sans-serif designs, solid and bold	A twentieth-century development	Based on shapes such as circles and squares	Inspired by Roman square capitals and serif forms
Mm	**Nn**	**Oo**	**Pp**
Caslon Egyptian	*Helvetica*	*Futura*	*Gill Sans*

Modulated	**Reverse Contrast**	**Rounded**	**Handwritten**
Thick verticals, thin horizontals	Thin verticals, thick horizontals	Friendly rounded corners	Designed to look hand-drawn
Qq	**Rr**	**Ss**	**Tt**
Britannic	*Antique Olive*	*Caslon Great Primer Rounded*	*Comic Sans*

* This is how sans-serif typefaces were first (inappropriately) described. 'The very shopboards must be [...] painted in Egyptian letters,' wrote Robert Southey in 1808, 'which, as the Egyptians had no letters, you will doubtless conceive must be curious. They are simply the common characters, deprived of all beauty and all proportion by having all the strokes of equal thickness.'

† The term 'grotesque', which was used at one time to describe all sans-serif typefaces, comes from the Italian *grottesco* ('cave-like') and refers to sans-serif Etruscan and Roman inscriptions that were discovered through excavation.

The SEVEN VOWELS

A vowel is a phonic sound made without constricting the lips, tongue, glottis or throat; they are the first sounds we learn to make as babies and they have traditionally been considered sacred. The seven Greek vowels were associated with the seven heavens. In Hebrew, vowels are unwritten but the seven sounds form the first of the seven names of God, יהוה (IEHΩOYA or 'Jehovah'), a name it is forbidden to pronounce.

A (alpha) · E (epsilon) · H (eta) · I (iota)

O (omicron) · Y (upsilon) · Ω (omega)

The BLOOMSBURY GROUP

In 1905, Thoby Stephen introduced his younger sisters, Vanessa and Virginia, to their future husbands, the writers Clive Bell and Leonard Woolf. They began to form a loose social circle in Bloomsbury, London, with the biographer Lytton Strachey and the economist John Maynard Keynes. They were a sexually tolerant group, about whom Dorothy Parker is said to have quipped: 'they lived in squares, painted in circles and loved in triangles'. Thoby was instrumental in bringing the group together, and instigated their regular 'Thursday Evenings', but he died in 1906 at the age of twenty-six after contracting typhoid while on holiday in Greece.

'OLD BLOOMSBURY'
Clive Bell · Vanessa Bell · E. M. Forster · Roger Fry
Duncan Grant · John Maynard Keynes · Desmond MacCarthy
Molly MacCarthy · Adrian Stephen · Karin Stephen · Lytton Strachey
Saxon Sydney-Turner · Leonard Woolf · Virginia Woolf

FRIENDS AND FAMILY
Angelica Bell · Julian Bell · Quentin Bell · Dora Carrington
Angelica Garnett · David Garnett · Lydia Lopokova
Ottoline Morrell · Frances Partridge · Vita Sackville-West
Alix Strachey · James Strachey · Julia Strachey · Arthur Waley

Some **AUTHORS** *who* **WROTE ONE NOVEL**

In 1935, the art critic Herbert Read published his only novel, *The Green Child*, about a faked assassination in South America and subterranean green people in Yorkshire. It is 'the kind of book to write if you are going to leave just the one novel behind', said the historian Geoffrey Wheatcroft: 'singular, odd, completely original'. Here are some more singular novels:

Le Grand Meaulnes	Alain-Fournier
Malina	Ingeborg Bachmann
Zuleika Dobson	Max Beerbohm
Two Serious Ladies	Jane Bowles
Wuthering Heights	Emily Brontë
The Shooting Party	Anton Chekhov
The Rock Pool	Cyril Connolly
All About H. Hatterr	G. V. Desani
Save Me the Waltz	Zelda Fitzgerald
The Other Side	Alfred Kubin
Dangerous Liaisons	Pierre Choderlos de Laclos
The Monk	Matthew Lewis
Focus	Arthur Miller
Gone With the Wind	Margaret Mitchell
Doctor Zhivago	Boris Pasternak
The Dwarfs	Harold Pinter
The Bell Jar	Sylvia Plath
The Narrative of Arthur Gordon Pym of Nantucket	Edgar Allan Poe
Ship of Fools	Katherine Anne Porter
The Notebooks of Malte Laurids Brigge	Rainer Maria Rilke
The Catcher in the Rye	J. D. Salinger
Black Beauty	Anna Sewell
Lord Malquist and Mr Moon	Tom Stoppard
The Leopard	Giuseppe Tomasi di Lampedusa
The Ragged Trousered Philanthropists	Robert Tressell
The Picture of Dorian Gray	Oscar Wilde

The PLATONIC SOLIDS

In Plato's *Timaeus*, the philosopher Timaeus of Locri describes the regular polyhedrons. He asserts that each of the four classical elements – earth, air, fire and water – is made up of atomic particles with these shapes. The dodecahedron, which, unlike the others, cannot be constructed from basic triangles, corresponds to a mysterious heavenly 'fifth element'.

TETRAHEDRON
'The pyramid [is] the solid figure that is the basic unit or seed of FIRE'

OCTAHEDRON
'We may regard the second of the figures we constructed as the basic unit of AIR'

ICOSAHEDRON
'The least sharp [...] the third of WATER'

CUBE
'Let us assign the cube to EARTH; for it is the most immobile of the four bodies and the most retentive of shape'

DODECAHEDRON
'A fifth construction, which the god used for arranging the constellations on the whole HEAVEN'

The OUTLAWS

Richmal Crompton's *Just William* books revolve around William's gang:

William · 'Ginger' · Henry · Douglas

William's surname is Brown; Ginger's is given as Flowerdew and elsewhere as Merridew; and although Henry and Douglas are not given surnames in the books, Crompton told a fan that they were Bates and Frinton.

The EARLY MODERN PLAYHOUSES of LONDON

The Theatre in Shoreditch was the first purpose-built theatre in England since Roman times, constructed by the actor James Burbage in open fields outside London. In 1594, Burbage founded the new Lord Chamberlain's Men, under the patronage of Henry Carey: the company included his own son Richard Burbage and a young William Shakespeare, and they performed at the Theatre and the Curtain. In 1598, following a dispute with the landlord, Richard Burbage deconstructed the Theatre and transported the beams south of the river to Southwark, where he built the Globe Theatre and the company continued to perform Shakespeare's plays. In 1603, King James VI and I became the company's patron and they changed their name to the King's Men. From 1608 they used Blackfriars as their winter playhouse. Here is a list of London's chief Elizabethan and Jacobean playhouses:

OUTDOOR THEATRES

The Red Lion, Whitechapel, 1567* · The Theatre, Shoreditch, 1576
Newington Butts, Southwark, 1576 · The Curtain, Shoreditch, 1577
The Rose, Southwark, 1587 · The Swan, Southwark, 1595
The Globe, Southwark, 1599 · The Fortune, Moorfields, 1600
The Hope, Southwark, 1613

INN-YARD THEATRES

The Bel Savage, Ludgate Hill, 1575 · The Bell, Gracechurch Street, 1576
The Cross Keys, Gracechurch Street, 1578 · The Bull, Bishopsgate Street, 1578
The Boar's Head, Whitechapel, 1598 · The Red Bull, Clerkenwell, 1604

INDOOR THEATRES

The Blackfriars Playhouse, Blackfriars, 1576 · The Whitefriars
Playhouse, Fleet Street, 1608 · The Cockpit Theatre, Drury Lane, 1616
The Porter's Hall Theatre, Blackfriars, 1616 · The Salisbury Court
Theatre, Fleet Street, 1629

In 1642, at the start of the Civil War, Parliament closed English theatres as being incompatible with the 'times of humiliation', and they remained closed until 1660.

---

* The Red Lion was a farm in Whitechapel, refitted as London's first dedicated theatre in 1567 by John Brayne, who was a wealthy grocer and James Burbage's brother-in-law. Its location was discovered by archaeologists in 2019.

INTERNATIONAL STANDARD BOOK NUMBERS

In 1965, W. H. Smith began building a computer-controlled warehouse in Swindon. They realized their operation needed a reliable book numbering system, so they commissioned Gordon Foster, a retired professor of statistics and former Bletchley Park codebreaker, to consider the problem. Foster devised a nine-digit system of unique 'Standard Book Numbers' (SBNs) and the International Organization for Standardization developed a ten-digit, international format (ISBN), which the UK adopted in 1974. ISBNs have had thirteen digits since 2007, when they were aligned with European Article Number (EAN) product codes. They have five elements:

'BOOK LAND' – European Article Numbers start with a three-digit 'Country Code', indicating an object's place of manufacture, but texts transcend national boundaries, so every book is allocated the arbitrary prefix 978 instead. This fictional 'country' is known affectionately as 'Book Land'. A new prefix – 979 – has recently been assigned to allow the expansion of Book Land; it is already in use in France.

LANGUAGE – This element can be a single digit: works in English are assigned '0' or '1'; '2' is for French; '3' for German; and '4' for Japanese. They can also be longer; works in Mongolian are assigned '99978'.

PUBLISHER – The third element relates to the publisher. For many years Penguin Books used '14'; Penguin Random House UK now uses '141' and '241'.

TITLE – The remaining digits (apart from the last one) represent each unique title. Nowadays these tend to be assigned at random, but Penguin Books once used the first three digits of this element to differentiate internal series: '020' for Pelican Books; '030' Puffin Books; and so on.

CHECK DIGIT – The final digit of the ISBN is known as the 'check digit' and is generated algorithmically from the others as a precaution against manual-entry errors. A computer system can use the check digit to assess whether an ISBN is genuine or not. To calculate a check digit, number an ISBN's digits from 13 on the left to 1 on the right. Add together all the digits in even positions and multiply the result by 3. Add to this the sum of all the digits in odd positions (except the check digit itself). Divide the result by 10. Discard the whole number, take the remainder and if it isn't zero subtract it from 10. The result is the check digit.

The RULES *of* DETECTIVE STORIES

The Catholic priest Ronald Knox made a new translation of the Bible and was appointed a 'protonotary apostolic' by the Pope. He was also the author of detective novels, including *The Viaduct Murder*, *The Body in the Silo* and *Double Cross Purposes*. In 1929, he wrote the introduction to an anthology of detective stories, in which he listed the 'Rules of Fair Play' (see also p.96).

1. The criminal must be someone mentioned in the early part of the story, but must not be anyone whose thoughts the reader has been allowed to follow.
2. All supernatural or preternatural agencies are ruled out as a matter of course.
3. Not more than one secret room or passage is allowable.
4. No hitherto undiscovered poisons may be used, nor any appliance which will need a long scientific explanation at the end.
5. No Chinaman must figure in the story.
6. No accident must ever help the detective, nor must he ever have an unaccountable intuition which proves to be right.
7. The detective must not himself commit the crime.
8. The detective must not light on any clues which are not instantly produced for the inspection of the reader.
9. The stupid friend of the detective, the Watson, must not conceal any thoughts which pass through his mind; his intelligence must be slightly, but very slightly, below that of the average reader.
10. Twin brothers, and doubles generally, must not appear unless we have been duly prepared for them.

Some LITERARY LINNAEANS

Some lucky animals have had literary Latin names bestowed upon them.

Anchylorhynchus pinocchio (a weevil) · *Baghcera kiplingi* (a jumping spider)
Desmodus draculae (a vampire bat) · *Iago garricki* (the longnose houndshark)
Nabokovia ada (a butterfly) · *Voeltzkowia mobydick* (a mermaid skink)

BEHIND BARS

'Even in prison,' wrote Oscar Wilde, 'a man can be quite free. His soul can be free.' A cell is both a physical restriction and a symbolic constraint, so, unsurprisingly, authors have often used prisons to explore the existential limits of human freedom. Here are twelve novels set in prison cells:

Springtime in a Broken Mirror by Mario Benedetti
The Stranger by Albert Camus
Falconer by John Cheever
The Enormous Room by e e cummings
The House of the Dead by Fyodor Dostoyevsky
I'm Not Stiller by Max Frisch
Miracle of the Rose by Jean Genet
Darkness at Noon by Arthur Koestler
Invitation to a Beheading by Vladimir Nabokov
The Tunnel by Ernesto Sabato
The Room by Hubert Selby Jr.
One Day in the Life of Ivan Denisovich by Aleksandr Solzhenitsyn

Doing time has one advantage at least: there is time to write. Imprisoned authors have often used their own prison sentences to write grand works of politics, philosophy, history or fiction. Here are twelve examples:

The Consolation of Philosophy by Boethius
The Pilgrim's Progress by John Bunyan
Don Quixote by Miguel de Cervantes
Memoirs of a Woman of Pleasure, or *Fanny Hill* by John Cleland*
The Story of My Experiments with Truth by M. K. Gandhi
Mein Kampf by Adolf Hitler
Conversations with Myself by Nelson Mandela
Devil on the Cross by Ngũgĩ wa Thiong'o
History of the World by Sir Walter Raleigh
An Introduction to Mathematical Philosophy by Bertrand Russell
De Profundis by Oscar Wilde
Tractatus Logico-Philosophicus by Ludwig Wittgenstein

---

* Cleland prepared *Fanny Hill* for publication while languishing in debtors' prison and it appeared just before his own release. When he got out, he was imprisoned again for having published such a scandalous novel: the erotic memoirs of a former prostitute.

The OBJECTS *that are* ON MY WORK-TABLE

Georges Perec's essay 'Notes Concerning the Objects that are on my Work-Table' is a list. 'Nothing seems easier than to draw up a list,' he says: 'in actual fact it's far more complicated than it appears; you always forget something, you are tempted to write, etc., but an inventory is when you don't write, etc.' Here are the items that are on his table:

my pen • a small round ashtray • pencils • paper • secateurs
folding rule • coffee cup • sealing wax • nail file • ammonite • a desk-lamp
a cigarette box • a bud-vase • a matchbox-holder • a cardboard box
containing little multi-coloured index-cards • a large *carton bouilli*
inkwell incrusted with tortoiseshell • a glass pencil-box
several stones • three hand-turned wooden boxes • an alarm-clock
a push-button calendar • a lump of lead • a large cigar box (with no
cigars in, but full of small objects) • a steel spiral into which you can
slide letters that are pending • a dagger handle of polished stone
account books • exercise books • loose sheets • multiple writing
instruments or accessories • a big hand-blotter • several books
a glass full of pencils • a small gilded wooden box

Some AUTHORS *who* WENT BLIND

IN ONE EYE
Gabriele D'Annunzio • Fyodor Dostoyevsky
Samuel Johnson • James Joyce • Carson McCullers
the Marquis de Sade • James Thurber* • Alice Walker

IN BOTH EYES
Jorge Luis Borges† • Benito Pérez Galdós • Homer • Aldous Huxley
Wyndham Lewis • John Milton • Oliver Sacks • Jean-Paul Sartre
Sue Townsend • William Wordsworth

* When Thurber was seven years old, his brother shot him in the eye with an arrow while they were playing a game of William Tell.
† With 'splendid irony', as he put it, Borges went blind in his fifties, just as he became the director of the National Library of Argentina, surrounded by books he would never read. (Strangely, Borges was the third blind librarian of the National Library of Argentina.)

The penultimate episode in James Joyce's *Ulysses* takes the form of an interrogation: short, clipped questions and imperatives are provided with pedantic responses, as Leopold Bloom makes cocoa for Stephen Dedalus and then makes his way to bed. The episode contains several exhaustive lists, such as the contents of Bloom's private drawer.

What did the first drawer unlocked contain?

A Vere Foster's handwriting copybook, property of Milly (Millicent) Bloom, certain pages of which bore diagram drawings marked *Papli*: which showed a large globular head with 5 hairs erect, 2 eyes in profile, the trunk full front with 3 large buttons, 1 triangular foot:

2 fading photographs of queen Alexandra of England and of Maud Branscombe, actress and professional beauty:

a Yuletide card, bearing on it a pictorial representation of a parasitic plant, the legend *Mizpah*, the date Xmas 1892, the name of the senders, from Mr and Mrs M. Comerford, the versicle: *May this Yuletide bring to thee, Joy and peace and welcome glee*:

a butt of red partly liquefied sealing wax, obtained from the stores department of Messrs Hely's, Ltd., 89, 90 and 91 Dame street:

a box containing the remainder of a gross of gilt «J» pennibs, obtained from same department of same firm:

an old sandglass which rolled containing sand which rolled:

a sealed prophecy (never unsealed) written by Leopold Bloom in 1886 concerning the consequences of the passing into law of William Ewart Gladstone's Home Rule bill of 1886 (never passed into law):

a bazaar ticket Nº 2004, of S. Kevin's Charity Fair, price 6d. 100 prizes:

an infantile epistle, dated, small em monday, reading: capital pee Papli comma capital aitch How are you note of interrogation capital eye I am very well full stop new paragraph signature with flourishes capital em Milly no stop:

a cameo brooch, property of Ellen Bloom (born Higgins), deceased:

3 typewritten letters, addressee, Henry Flower, c/o P. O. Westland Row, addresser, Martha Clifford, c/o P. O. Dolphin's Barn:

the transliterated name and address of the addresser of the 3 letters in reserved alphabetic boustrophedontic punctated quadrilinear cryptogram (vowels suppressed) N. IGS./WI. UU. OX/W. OKS. MH/Y. IM:

a press cutting from an English weekly periodical *Modern Society*, subject corporal chastisement in girls' schools:

a pink ribbon which had festooned an Easter egg in the year 1899:

two partly uncoiled rubber preservatives with reserve pockets, purchased by post from Box 32, P. O., Charing Cross, London, W. C.:

1 pack of 1 dozen creamlaid envelopes and faintruled notepaper, watermarked, now reduced by 3:

some assorted Austrian-Hungarian coins:

2 coupons of the Royal and Privileged Hungarian Lottery:

a low-power magnifying glass:

2 erotic photocards showing: a) buccal coition between nude senorita (rere presentation, superior position) and nude torero (fore presentation, inferior position): b) anal violation by male religious (fully clothed, eyes abject) of female religious (partly clothed, eyes direct), purchased by post from Box 32, P. O., Charing Cross, London, W. C.:

a press cutting of recipe for renovation of old tan boots:

a 1d. adhesive stamp, lavender, of the reign of Queen Victoria:

a chart of measurements of Leopold Bloom compiled before, during and after 2 months of consecutive use of Sandow-Whiteley's pulley exerciser (men's 15/-, athlete's 20/-) viz., chest 28 in and 29 1/2 in, biceps 9 in and 10 in, forearm 8 1/2 and 9 in, thigh 10 in and 12 in, calf 11 in and 12 in:

1 prospectus of the Wonderworker, the world's greatest remedy for rectal complaints direct from Wonderworker, Coventry House, South Place, London E. C., addressed to Mrs L. Bloom with brief accompanying note commencing: Dear Madam.

The SEVEN TYPES *of* AMBIGUITY

As a Cambridge undergraduate, the poet William Empson began thinking about literary 'ambiguity', writing which allows for alternative readings. In 1930, at the age of twenty-four, he published *Seven Types of Ambiguity*, which became a foundational work of twentieth-century literary criticism.

FIRST-type ambiguities arise when a detail is effective in several ways at once. ¶ In SECOND-type ambiguities two or more alternative meanings are fully resolved into one. ¶ The condition for THIRD-type ambiguity is that two apparently unconnected meanings are given simultaneously. ¶ In the FOURTH type the alternative meanings combine to make clear a complicated state of mind in the author. ¶ The FIFTH type is a fortunate confusion, as when the author is discovering his idea in the act of writing or not holding it all in mind at once. ¶ In the SIXTH type what is said is contradictory or irrelevant and the reader is forced to invent interpretations. ¶ The SEVENTH type is that of full contradiction, marking a division in the author's mind.

The CHOCOLATE FACTORY

As a schoolchild, Roald Dahl and his friends frequently tested confections from the local Cadbury's chocolate factory. Dahl later wrote *Charlie and the Chocolate Factory* about a boy who gets to visit the factory of the genius chocolatier Willy Wonka, who has a number of remarkable products.

Blue Birds' Eggs • Butterscotch and Buttergin • Cavity-Filling Caramels
The Chewing-Gum Meal • Colour-Changing Caramels • Everlasting
Gobstoppers • Fizzy Lifting Drinks • Hair Toffee • Hot Ice Creams for
Cold Days • Lickable Wallpaper for Nurseries • Magic Hand-Fudge*
Nutty Crunch Surprise • Rainbow Drops† • Stickjaw for Talkative
Parents • Strawberry-Juice Water Pistols • Sugar Balloons • Swudge Grass
Whipple Scrumptious Fudgemallow Delight • Wriggle-Sweets

---

* 'When You Hold It in Your Hand, You Taste It in Your Mouth.'
† 'Suck them and You Can Spit in Six Different Colours.'

CHANDLER'S ONE-LINERS

Raymond Chandler's hard-boiled investigator, Philip Marlowe, is famous for his deadpan narration, in novels such as *The Big Sleep*, *The High Window*, *The Little Sister* and *The Long Good-bye*. Here are some of his best lines about the blondes and bruisers he meets in the noir streets of Los Angeles.

It was a blonde. A blonde to make a bishop kick a hole in a stained-glass window.

The voice that answered was fat. It wheezed softly, like the voice of a man who had just won a pie-eating contest.

She gave me a smile that I could feel in my hip pocket.

The kid's face had as much expression as a cut of round steak and was about the same colour.

From thirty feet away she looked like a lot of class. From ten feet away she looked like something made up to be seen from thirty feet away.

The General spoke again, slowly, using his strength as carefully as an out-of-work show-girl uses her last pair of stockings.

Her smile was as faint as a fat lady at a fireman's ball.

His smile was as stiff as a frozen fish.

She smelled the way the Taj Mahal looks by moonlight.

Even on Central Avenue, not the quietest dressed street in the world, he looked about as inconspicuous as a tarantula on a slice of angel food.

To say she had a face that would have stopped a clock would have been an insult to her. It would have stopped a runaway horse.

He had a battered face that looked as if it had been hit by everything but the bucket of a dragline.

The girl gave him a look which ought to have stuck at least four inches out of his back.

He was a guy who talked with commas, like a heavy novel. Over the phone anyway.

RULES *for* PARENTS

In September 1959, Susan Sontag compiled this list in her notebook. Her only son, David Rieff, who was aged seven at the time, edited her journals and included it in *Reborn: Early Diaries, Journals and Notebooks* (2009).

1. Be consistent.
2. Don't speak about him to others (e.g., tell funny things) in his presence. (Don't make him self-conscious.)
3. Don't praise him for something I wouldn't always accept as good.
4. Don't reprimand him harshly for something he's been allowed to do.
5. Daily routine: eating, homework, bath, teeth, room, story, bed.
6. Don't allow him to monopolize me when I am with other people.
7. Always speak well of his pop. (No faces, sighs, impatience, etc.)
8. Do not discourage childish fantasies.
9. Make him aware that there is a grown-up world that's none of his business.
10. Don't assume that what I don't like to do (bath, hairwash) he won't like either.

BURNED BOOKS

'That was but a prelude; where they burn books, they will ultimately burn people as well.' This line from Heinrich Heine's 1821 play *Almansor* marks the spot in Berlin's Bebelplatz where one of the first major Nazi book burnings took place, on 10 May 1933. Works by these authors were burned by the Nazis during the course of the following decade:

Walter Benjamin · Bertolt Brecht · Joseph Conrad · John Dos Passos
Fyodor Dostoyevsky · F. Scott Fitzgerald · Sigmund Freud · André Gide
Ernest Hemingway · Hermann Hesse · Victor Hugo · Aldous Huxley
James Joyce · Franz Kafka · D. H. Lawrence · Jack London · Thomas Mann
Vladimir Nabokov · Erich Maria Remarque · Joseph Roth
Arthur Schnitzler · Upton Sinclair · Leo Tolstoy · Mark Twain
H. G. Wells · Walt Whitman · Oscar Wilde · and many others

Mr LEAR'S LADIES and GENTLEMEN

The origins of the limerick are obscure, but the form was popularized by the poet and painter Edward Lear in his *Book of Nonsense* (1846) and its sequels, which he illustrated himself. Most of Lear's limericks feature old men or young ladies, as in the following selection of opening couplets:

There was an Old Man with a beard,
Who said, 'It is just as I feared!'*

There was an Old Man on some rocks,
Who shut his Wife up in a box

There was an Old Man who said, 'How
Shall I flee from this horrible Cow?'

There was an Old Man of Jamaica,
Who suddenly married a Quaker

There was an Old Man of the Coast,
Who placidly sat on a post

There was an Old Man who supposed
That the street door was partially closed

There was an Old Man in a boat,
Who said, 'I'm afloat! I'm afloat!'

There was an Old Man of Whitehaven,
Who danced a quadrille with a Raven

There was an Old Man of Quebec,
A beetle ran over his neck

There was an Old Man of Vesuvius,
Who studied the works of Vitruvius

There was an Old Person whose habits
Induced him to feed upon Rabbits

There was a Young Lady of Troy,
Whom several large flies did annoy

There was a Young Lady whose chin
Resembled the point of a pin

There was a Young Lady of Wales,
Who caught a large Fish without scales

There was a Young Lady whose nose
Was so long that it reached to her toes

There was a Young Lady of Norway,
Who casually sat in a doorway

There was a Young Girl of Majorca,
Whose Aunt was a very fast walker

There was a Young Lady of Lucca,
Whose lovers completely forsook her

There was a Young Lady whose eyes
Were unique as to colour and size

There was a Young Lady of Clare,
Who was sadly pursued by a Bear

There was a Young Lady of Ryde,
Whose shoe-strings were seldom untied

There was a Young Lady whose bonnet
Came untied when the birds sate upon it

---

* Limericks are often obscene, though Lear's are not. Another slight disappointment is that Lear tends to repeat the last word of the first line as the last word of the limerick, missing the opportunity for an amusing rhyme. This tendency was satirized by the comedian John Clarke, who wrote the following limerick: 'There was an old man with a beard / A funny old man with a beard / He had a big beard / A great big old beard / That amusing old man with a beard.'

Some SUBTITLES

In 1765, Horace Walpole published his only novel, *The Castle of Otranto*, with the subtitle *A Gothic Story*. This was one of the first times the word 'gothic' had been attached to a work of literature and his subtitle founded a new genre of tales of terror, involving crumbling castles, secret passageways and family curses. Here are some more subtitles (see also p.27):

The Hunting of the Snark	*An Agony in Eight Fits*	Lewis Carroll
Jane Eyre	*An Autobiography*	Charlotte Brontë
Thus Spoke Zarathustra	*A Book for Everyone and No One*	Friedrich Nietzsche
Animal Farm	*A Fairy Story*	George Orwell
The Man Who Was Thursday	*A Nightmare*	G. K. Chesterton
Vanity Fair	*A Novel Without a Hero*	W. M. Thackeray
The Secret Agent	*A Simple Tale*	Joseph Conrad
Middlemarch	*A Study of Provincial Life*	George Eliot
Money	*A Suicide Note*	Martin Amis
The Good Soldier	*A Tale of Passion*	Ford Madox Ford

THINGS *that* MAKE YOUR HEART BEAT FASTER

Sei Shōnagon was a gentlewoman at the court of the Empress Consort Teishi in tenth-century Japan, and the author of *The Pillow Book*, a collection of observations written on a sheaf of paper that she kept by her pillow. She includes anecdotes, poems and many lists, such as this one:

A sparrow with nestlings. ¶ Going past a place where tiny children are playing. ¶ Lighting some fine incense and then lying down alone to sleep. ¶ Looking into a Chinese mirror that's a little clouded. ¶ A fine gentleman pulls up in his carriage and sends in some request. ¶ To wash your hair, apply your makeup and put on clothes that are well-scented with incense. Even if you're somewhere where no one special will see you, you still feel a heady sense of pleasure inside. ¶ On a night when you're waiting for someone to come, there's a sudden gust of rain and something rattles in the wind, making your heart suddenly beat faster.

PYGMIES, PALMS *and* PIRATES

Of pygmies, palms and pirates,
Of islands and lagoons,
Of blood-bespattered frigates,
Of crags and octoroons,
Of whales and broken bottles,
Of quicksands cold and grey,
Of ullages and dottles,
I have no more to say.

Of barley, corn and furrows,
Of farms and turf that heaves
Above such ghostly burrows
As twitch on summer eves,
Of fallow-land and pasture,
Of skies both pink and grey,
I made a statement last year
And have no more to say.

from *A Book of Nonsense* by Mervyn Peake

The HOUSE *of* ATREUS

Of the thirty-two ancient Greek tragedies that survive, thirteen involve members of the House of Atreus, a treacherous and adulterous clan, whose murderous machinations provide rich dramatic material.

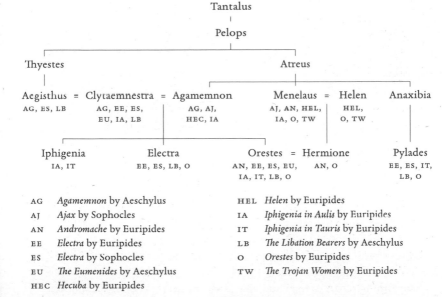

Tantalus
|
Pelops

Thyestes — Atreus

Aegisthus = Clytaemnestra = Agamemnon   Menelaus = Helen   Anaxibia
AG, ES, LB   AG, EE, ES,   AG, AJ,   AJ, AN, HEL,   HEL,
EU, IA, LB   HEC, IA   IA, O, TW   O, TW

Iphigenia   Electra   Orestes = Hermione   Pylades
IA, IT   EE, ES, LB, O   AN, EE, ES, EU,   AN, O   EE, ES, IT,
IA, IT, LB, O   LB, O

AG	*Agamemnon* by Aeschylus	HEL	*Helen* by Euripides
AJ	*Ajax* by Sophocles	IA	*Iphigenia in Aulis* by Euripides
AN	*Andromache* by Euripides	IT	*Iphigenia in Tauris* by Euripides
EE	*Electra* by Euripides	LB	*The Libation Bearers* by Aeschylus
ES	*Electra* by Sophocles	O	*Orestes* by Euripides
EU	*The Eumenides* by Aeschylus	TW	*The Trojan Women* by Euripides
HEC	*Hecuba* by Euripides		

The ABSURD OPINION *of* GENTILISME

In his political treatise *Leviathan*, Thomas Hobbes rails against pre-Christian 'gentiles' and their tendency to worship almost anything as either a god or a 'divel'. The novelist William H. Gass, in 'I've Got a Little List', an essay on the art of literary list-writing, declared this passage to be 'one of the great lists in our language,' full of 'admirable wealth and energy'.

The unformed matter of the World, was a God, by the name of *Chaos*.

The Heaven, the Ocean, the Planets, the Fire, the Earth, the Winds, were so many Gods.

Men, Women, a Bird, a Crocodile, a Calf, a Dogge, a Snake, an Onion, a Leeke, Deified.

Besides, that they filled almost all places, with spirits called *Daemons*: the plains, with *Pan*, and *Panises*, or Satyres;

the Woods, with Fawnes, and Nymphs;

the Sea, with Tritons, and other Nymphs;

every River, and Fountayn, with a Ghost of his name, and with Nymphs;

every house, with its *Lares*, or Familiars;

every man, with his *Genius*;

Hell, with Ghosts, and spirituall Officers, as *Charon*, *Cerberus*, and the *Furies*;

and in the night time, all places with *Larvae*, *Lemures*, Ghosts of men deceased, and a whole kingdome of Fayries, and Bugbears.

They have also ascribed Divinity, and built Temples to meer Accidents, and Qualities; such as are Time, Night, Day, Peace, Concord, Love, Contention, Vertue, Honour, Health, Rust, Fever, and the like; which when they prayed for, or against, they prayed to, as if there were Ghosts of those names hanging over their heads, and letting fall, or withholding that Good, or Evill, for, or against which they prayed.

They invoked also their own Wit, by the name of *Muses* (see p.76);

their own Ignorance, by the name of *Fortune*;

their own Lust, by the name of *Cupid*;

their own Rage, by the name *Furies*;

their own privy members by the name of *Priapus*;

and attributed their pollutions, to *Incubi*, and *Succubae*:

insomuch as there was nothing, which a Poet could introduce as a person in his Poem, which they did not make either a *God*, or a *Divel*.

The HUNDRED and ONE DALMATIANS

Pongo · Missis · Perdita · Prince
Patch · Lucky · Cadpig · Roly Poly
and ninety-three other pups

DRINKING UNDER the VOLCANO

In Malcolm Lowry's *Under the Volcano*, Geoffrey Firmin is an alcoholic former British consul in Mexico. The novel is set over the course of a single day – the Day of the Dead, 2 November 1938 – and the volcano of the title is Popocatépetl, which looms over the town of Quauhnahuac. Firmin drinks himself into oblivion, experiencing 'moments of translucent clairvoyance', as Stephen Spender put it. This is his schedule:

7 a.m. a 'long shuddering' whisky at the Bella Vista bar

7.30 a few slugs of sweet quince wine in a small shop on Calle Tierra del Fuego

9 a.m. a 'long draught' of Burke's Irish whiskey on Calle Nicaragua

9.45 half a tumbler of mescal and a 'fierce' drink of Johnny Walker

10.30 a long, deep drink from the tequila bottle

11.30 at least two bottles of Carta Blanca beer

12.30 'a stiff drink' from a bathroom toothmug, and then another

1.30 one cocktail, the remains of three others and the rest of the shaker at Jacques's house

1.50 two glasses of tequila at the Paris Café

2.10 three glasses of tequila at the Terminal Cantina El Bosque

3.15 a 'short drink' of habanero on the bus to Tomalin

3.45 the rest of the bottle of habanero at Arena Tomalin

4.30 two 'small mescals' and at least one beer at the Salón Ofélia in Tomalin

6 p.m. six mescals, the rest of bottle, two more mescals, and then 'everything in sight' at El Farolito, Parián

Some AIRPORTS NAMED *after* AUTHORS

Antoine de Saint-Exupéry liked to write and read in his aeroplane cockpit and once circled an airfield for an hour while finishing an exciting novel.

AIMÉ CÉSAIRE airport, Martinique · ARISTOTELIS airport, Kastoria, Greece · IAN FLEMING airport, Boscobel, Jamaica IBN BATOUTA airport, Tangier, Morocco · MARCO POLO airport, Venice, Italy · SAINT EXUPÉRY airport, Lyon, France · VÁCLAV HAVEL airport, Prague, Czech Republic WŁADYSŁAW REYMONT airport, Łódź, Poland

The SURREALIST VOICE

'A good number of poets could pass for Surrealists,' wrote André Breton, 'beginning with Dante and, in his finer moments, Shakespeare.' He goes on to list more writers who have demonstrated aspects of Surrealism:*

SWIFT is Surrealist in malice. ¶ SADE is Surrealist in sadism. ¶ CHATEAUBRIAND is Surrealist in exoticism. ¶ CONSTANT is Surrealist in politics. ¶ HUGO is Surrealist when he isn't stupid. ¶ DESBORDES-VALMORE is Surrealist in love. ¶ BERTRAND is Surrealist in the past. ¶ RABBE is Surrealist in death. ¶ POE is Surrealist in adventure. ¶ BAUDELAIRE is Surrealist in morality. ¶ RIMBAUD is Surrealist in the way he lived, and elsewhere. ¶ MALLARMÉ is Surrealist when he is confiding. ¶ JARRY is Surrealist in absinthe. ¶ NOUVEAU is Surrealist in the kiss. ¶ SAINT-POL-ROUX is Surrealist in his use of symbols. ¶ FARGUE is Surrealist in the atmosphere. ¶ VACHÉ is Surrealist in me.† ¶ REVERDY is Surrealist at home. ¶ SAINT-JEAN-PERSE is Surrealist at a distance. ¶ ROUSSEL is Surrealist as a storyteller.   *Etc.*

---

* In the first *Manifesto of Surrealism*, from which the list above is taken, Breton defined Surrealism as 'psychic automatism in its pure state, by which one proposed to express – verbally, by means of the written word, or in any other manner – the actual functioning of thought.'

† Breton once said that his friend Jacques Vaché had been his principal literary inspiration. Vaché died in 1919 of an opium overdose, at the age of twenty-three, five years before Breton wrote the *Manifesto of Surrealism*.

The world's earliest recorded joke was written in Sumerian in 1900 BC and translates roughly as: 'Something which has never occurred since time immemorial; a young woman did not fart in her husband's lap.' Literature has had a ripe history of fart humour ever since.

The Clouds by Aristophanes

If a little tummy like yours can create a fart like that, is it surprising that from an infinity of air you can get a mighty roll of thunder?

Inferno by Dante Alighieri

Each poked a tongue, teeth clenched, towards their lord,
and he – to give the order now, "Quick march!" –
in answer made a trumpet of his arse.

The Miller's Tale by Geoffrey Chaucer

"Spek, sweete bryd, I noot nat where thou art."
This Nicholas anon leet fle a fart.

Gargantua by François Rabelais

With the fart that he let the earth trembled nine leagues.

The Comedy of Errors by William Shakespeare

A man may break a word with you, sir; and words are but wind;
Ay, and break it in your face, so he break it not behind.

The Benefit of Farting Explained by Jonathan Swift

Wrote in Spanish by Don Fartinando Puff-indorst, Professor of Bumbast in the University of Crackow, and translated into English at his request.

Molloy by Samuel Beckett

Four farts every fifteen minutes. It's nothing. Not even one fart every four minutes. It's unbelievable. Damn it, I hardly fart at all.

The Catcher in the Rye by J. D. Salinger

This guy sitting in the row in front of me, Edgar Marsalla, laid this terrific fart. It was a very crude thing to do, in the chapel and all, but it was quite amusing. Old Marsalla. He damn near blew the roof off.

LOOKING-GLASS CHESS

'Chess problems,' wrote Vladimir Nabokov, 'demand from the composer the same virtues that characterize all worthwhile art: originality, invention, conciseness, harmony, complexity, and splendid insincerity.' In *Through the Looking-Glass* by Lewis Carroll, the countryside is marked out like a chessboard, divided by brooks and hedges. Alice joins a game in progress and the story becomes the elaborate solution to a chess problem – which Carroll printed at the start of the book:

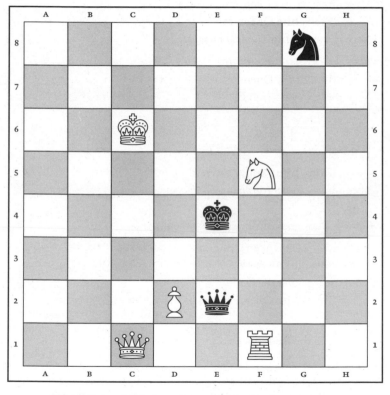

White Pawn (Alice) to play, and win in eleven moves.

Carroll also provided the solution, in which, he admits, 'the *alternation* of Red and White is perhaps not so strictly observed as it might be', but he confirms that the checkmate is 'strictly in accordance with the laws of the game'. Carroll's solution maps on to the *Looking-Glass* chapters as follows:

2. THE GARDEN OF LIVE FLOWERS

Alice meets the Red Queen and takes the place of the pawn Lily (D2)*

The Red Queen moves to H5

3. LOOKING-GLASS INSECTS

Alice moves through D3 (*by railway*) to D4 (*Tweedledum and Tweedledee*)

5. WOOL AND WATER

The White Queen moves to C4 (*chasing her shawl*)

Alice meets the White Queen (*with shawl*)

The White Queen moves to C5 (*becomes sheep*)

Alice moves to D5 (*shop, river, shop*)

The White Queen moves to F8 (*leaves egg on shelf*)

Alice moves to D6 (*Humpty Dumpty*)

7. THE LION AND THE UNICORN

The White Queen moves to C8 (*flying from Red Knight*)

Alice moves to D7 (*forest*)

8. 'IT'S MY OWN INVENTION'

The Red Knight moves to E7 (check)

The White Knight takes Red Knight

The White Knight moves to F5

Alice moves to D8 (*coronation*)

9. QUEEN ALICE

The Red Queen moves to E8 (*examination*)

Alice becomes a Queen

The Queens 'castle'†

Alice castles (*joins the feast*)

The White Queen moves to A6 (*into the soup tureen*)

10. SHAKING

Alice takes the Red Queen and wins (checkmate)

The only chess pieces that don't feature in *Through the Looking-Glass* are the bishops, although a white bishop can be seen reading a newspaper in one of John Tenniel's illustrations. In 1974, Isaac Asimov wrote 'The Curious Omission', a mystery story inspired by Carroll's omission of the bishops.

---

* 'Carroll does a remarkable job,' writes Martin Gardner in his *Annotated Alice*. 'At no time, for example, does Alice exchange words with a piece that is not then on a square alongside her own.'

† There is no chess move in which queens castle, but Carroll explained: 'The "castling" of the three Queens is merely a way of saying that they entered the palace.'

Some UNUSUAL DEATHS

C. S. Lewis died in Oxford on the same day as Aldous Huxley in Los Angeles, 22 November 1963, but both their deaths were overshadowed by the death of President John F. Kennedy, assassinated that same day in Dallas. Here are some more authors who died in unusual circumstances:

Sherwood Anderson	died of peritonitis of the colon after swallowing a toothpick.
Pietro Aretino	died of suffocation from laughing too much.
Francis Bacon	died of pneumonia after stuffing a chicken with snow as an experiment.
Arnold Bennett	died of typhoid after drinking tap water in a French restaurant.
Anton Chekhov	died while drinking champagne; he was transported home in an ice-car intended for oysters.
Epicurus	died sitting in a warm bath with a cup of wine in his hand.
Ödön von Horváth	was killed by a falling branch on the Champs-Élysées.
Li Po	drowned attempting to grasp the moon's reflection.
Christopher Marlowe	died in Deptford after being stabbed in the eye.
Pliny the Elder	died attempting to save a friend from the same eruption of Mount Vesuvius that buried Pompeii.
Alexander Pushkin	died in a duel with his brother-in-law.
Rainer Maria Rilke	pricked his finger whilst gathering roses; it became infected and he never recovered.
Robert Louis Stevenson	died in Samoa while making a batch of mayonnaise.
St Teresa of Ávila	died on the night that the Julian calendar was replaced with the Gregorian calendar in Spain.*
Leo Tolstoy	died in a small train station, while running away from his wife at the age of eighty-two.
Mark Twain	was born soon after the 1835 appearance of Halley's Comet and predicted he would 'go out with it as well'; he died the day after the comet reappeared in 1910.
Boris Vian	died of a heart attack while attending an unsatisfactory film adaptation of his novel *I Will Spit on Your Graves*.
Tennessee Williams	choked on the cap of a bottle of pills.

* Ten days were 'lost' at midnight on this night, so the date of her death is uncertain: it was either 4 October or 15 October 1582.

La RONDE

Arthur Schnitzler's play *Reigen*, or *La Ronde* ('the round dance'), has ten scenes. Each scene is a conversation between two lovers, just before or just after sex, and each features one character from the previous scene, so that they form a sexual circle. Schnitzler wrote the play in 1897 and it caused a moral scandal when it was performed in 1920. In *The Blue Room*, David Hare's 1998 adaptation, Nicole Kidman and Iain Glen played all the roles.

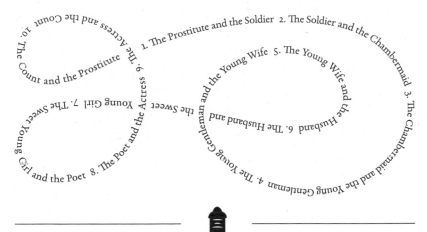

STRANGERS *in* PÈRE LACHAISE

Père Lachaise Cemetery in Paris is the most visited necropolis in the world, famous for its many tombs of French writers, including Honoré de Balzac, Colette, Molière and Marcel Proust. The cemetery is also home to a number of authors who died in Paris, but were from elsewhere:

Chantal Akerman · Miguel Ángel Asturias* · Ludwig Börne
Nancy Cunard · Enrique Gómez Carrillo · Sadeq Hedayat
Stuart Merrill · Jim Morrison · Cyprian Norwid · Georges Rodenbach
Shahan Shahnour · Gertrude Stein · Alice B. Toklas · Oscar Wilde
Helen Maria Williams · Richard Wright

* The Guatemalan novelist and diplomat Miguel Ángel Asturias won the Nobel Prize in 1967. He is best remembered for his novel *The President*, about life under a ruthless dictator of an anonymous South American state.

TRAGIC ENDS

The first Greek tragedy was written in the sixth century BC by Thespis, who was awarded a prize goat. This may be the origin of the word tragedy, which means 'goat-song'. Thereafter Greek tragedians composed trilogies of tragedies, which were performed at the festival of Dionysus in Athens. The tragedies that survive feature a range of gruesome deaths, from matricide and parricide to infanticide and suicide, involving poisonous shirts, wild horses, child sacrifice and frenzied dismemberment. The three greatest tragedians are said to have met appropriately tragic ends.

Aeschylus   was struck by a falling tortoise, dropped by an eagle.

Sophocles   expired attempting to recite a lengthy line from his own play *Antigone* without pausing for breath.

Euripides   was ripped apart by the King of Macedon's Molossian hounds after living in a cave for most of his life.

The BEAT GENERATION

Jack Kerouac suggested the term 'Beat Generation' while talking with John Clellon Holmes in 1948. 'More than mere weariness, it implies the feeling of having been used, of being raw,' wrote Holmes. 'It involves a sort of nakedness of mind, and, ultimately, of soul: a feeling of being reduced to the bedrock of consciousness.' The central Beat writers met in New York in the early 1940s; their key works include *On the Road* by Jack Kerouac, *Howl* by Allen Ginsberg and *Naked Lunch* by William S. Burroughs.

CENTRAL BEATS
William S. Burroughs · Lucien Carr · Neal Cassady · Allen Ginsberg
John Clellon Holmes · Herbert Huncke · Jack Kerouac

LATER BEATS
Gregory Corso · Philip Lamentia · Michael McClure · Peter Orlovsky
Gary Snyder · Carl Solomon · Philip Whalen

UNFINISHED BUSINESS

These novelists were working on books when they died, which have since been published posthumously and unfinished. In more than one case, subsequent authors have completed the novels: Frederick Greenwood wrote the final instalment of *Wives and Daughters*; Robert B. Parker finished *Poodle Springs*; and Thomas Power James, an American spiritualist, completed a literally ghost-written edition of Charles Dickens's *The Mystery of Edwin Drood* by taking dictation from beyond the grave.

Laurence Sterne	d. 1768	*A Sentimental Journey through France and Italy*	pub. 1768
Mary Wollstonecraft	d. 1797	*Maria, or The Wrongs of Woman*	pub. 1798
Jane Austen	d. 1817	*Sanditon*	pub. 1925
Elizabeth Gaskell	d. 1865	*Wives and Daughters*	pub. 1866
Charles Dickens	d. 1870	*The Mystery of Edwin Drood*	pub. 1870
Gustave Flaubert	d. 1880	*Bouvard and Pécuchet*	pub. 1881
Robert Louis Stevenson	d. 1894	*The Weir of Hermiston*	pub. 1896
Natsume Sōseki	d. 1916	*Light and Darkness*	pub. 1917
Henry James	d. 1916	*The Ivory Tower*	pub. 1917
Joseph Conrad	d. 1924	*Suspense*	pub. 1925
Franz Kafka	d. 1924	*The Castle*	pub. 1926
Edith Wharton	d. 1937	*The Buccaneers*	pub. 1938
Mikhail Bulgakov	d. 1940	*A Dead Man's Memoir*	pub. 1965
F. Scott Fitzgerald	d. 1940	*The Last Tycoon*	pub. 1941
Robert Musil	d. 1942	*The Man Without Qualities*	pub. 1943
Ernest Hemingway	d. 1946	*The Garden of Eden*	pub. 1986
Raymond Chandler	d. 1959	*Poodle Springs*	pub. 1962
Albert Camus	d. 1960	*The First Man*	pub. 1994
Vladimir Nabokov	d. 1977	*The Original of Laura* *	pub. 2009
Ralph Ellison	d. 1994	*Juneteenth*	pub. 1999
David Foster Wallace	d. 2008	*The Pale King*	pub. 2011

* Nabokov's dying wish was that his unfinished novel should be destroyed, but it was placed in a Swiss bank vault and thirty years later it was published. The manuscript, written on index cards, concludes with a list: 'efface, expunge, erase, delete, rub out, wipe out, obliterate'.

REST *in* PEACE

'And were an epitaph to be my story,' wrote Robert Frost, 'I'd have a short one ready for my own. / I would have written of me on my stone: / I had a lover's quarrel with the world.' Here are some more authors' epitaphs:

Aphra Behn	Here lies a Proof that Wit can never be Defence enough against Mortality
Joseph Conrad	Sleep after toyle, port after stormie seas, Ease after warre, death after life, does greatly please.*
Emily Dickinson	Called Back
F. Scott Fitzgerald	So we beat on, boats against the current, borne back ceaselessly into the past†
John Keats	Here lies One Whose Name was writ in Water.
Spike Milligan	Duirt mé leat go raibh mé breoite [I told you I was ill]
Dorothy Parker	Excuse my dust.
Sylvia Plath	Even amidst fierce flames the golden lotus can be planted‡
William Shakespeare	Good Friend, for Jesus' sake forbear To dig the dust enclosed here. Blessed be the man that spares these stones, And curst be he that moves my bones.
Percy Bysshe Shelley	Nothing of him that doth fade But doth suffer a sea-change Into something rich and strange§
Virginia Woolf	Against you I will fling myself, unvanquished and unyielding, O Death!‖
W. B. Yeats	Cast a cold Eye On Life, on Death Horseman, pass by!¶

---

* from *The Faerie Queene* by Edmund Spenser
† the last line of *The Great Gatsby*
‡ from *Monkey* by Wu Ch'eng-En (see p.30)
§ from *The Tempest* by William Shakespeare
‖ from *The Waves*
¶ from 'Under Bel Bulben'

The LONELY HEARTS CLUB

Designed by Peter Blake and Jann Haworth, the front cover of the 1967 Beatles album *Sgt. Pepper's Lonely Hearts Club Band* features a montage of seventy-one figures, including the following authors:

William S. Burroughs · Lewis Carroll · Stephen Crane
Aleister Crowley · Bob Dylan · Aldous Huxley · James Joyce · Carl Jung
T. E. Lawrence · Karl Marx · Edgar Allan Poe · George Bernard Shaw
Terry Southern · Dylan Thomas · H. G. Wells · Oscar Wilde

The FUTURE LIBRARY

The Scottish artist Katie Paterson has planted 1,000 trees in Nordmarka, a forest in southern Norway. Each year a different writer contributes a text to the Future Library, to be held in trust, unpublished, until 2114, at which point the 100 books will be printed on paper made from the trees. For the time being, the manuscripts are held at the Deichman Library in Oslo, in a 'Silent Room' panelled with wood from the same forest. 'Future Library is a living, breathing, organic artwork, unfolding over one hundred years,' says Paterson. 'It will live and breathe through the material growth of the trees – I imagine the tree rings as chapters in a book.' Eight authors have so far donated texts:

2014	Margaret Atwood
2015	David Mitchell
2016	Sjón*
2017	Elif Shafak
2018	Han Kang
2019	Karl Ove Knausgaard
2020	Ocean Vuong
2021	Tsitsi Dangarembga

* Some of the authors have revealed the titles of their books. Margaret Atwood's is called *Scribbler Moon*; David Mitchell's is *From Me Flows What You Call Time*; while the Icelandic novelist Sjón has written a book called *As My Brow Brushes On the Tunics of Angels, or The Drop Tower, the Roller Coaster, the Whirling Cups and other Instruments of Worship from the Post-Industrial Age.*

FAMOUS LAST WORDS

In the game *Ex Libris*, players flip a coin to decide whether they must invent the opening or closing sentence of a book. Closing lines are often harder to write convincingly, because they need to imply an entire preceding narrative. Here are some of the greatest closing lines in literature.

I don't know, I'll never know, in the silence you don't know, you must go on, I can't go on, I'll go on.
— *The Unnamable* by Samuel Beckett

It is a far, far better thing that I do, than I have ever done; it is a far, far better rest that I go to than I have ever known.
— *A Tale of Two Cities* by Charles Dickens

Silence lay steadily against the wood and stone of Hill House, and whatever walked there, walked alone.
— *The Haunting of Hill House* by Shirley Jackson

'Like a dog!' he said. It was as if the shame would outlive him.
— *The Trial* by Franz Kafka

Somebody threw a dead dog after him down the ravine.
— *Under the Volcano* by Malcolm Lowry

He loved Big Brother. — *Nineteen Eighty-Four* by George Orwell

Only the margin left to write on now. I love you, I love you, I love you.
— *I Capture the Castle* by Dodie Smith

L—d! said my mother, what is all this story about?——A COCK and a BULL, said Yorick——And one of the best of its kind, I ever heard.
— *Tristram Shandy* by Laurence Sterne

Come children, let us shut up the box and the puppets, for our play is played out.
— *Vanity Fair* by William Makepeace Thackeray

'That is well put,' replied Candide, 'but we must cultivate our garden.'
— *Candide* by Voltaire

It was done; it was finished. Yes, she thought, laying down her brush in extreme fatigue, I have had my vision.
— *To the Lighthouse* by Virginia Woolf

An INDEX

'I'm always embarrassed when I see an index an author has made of his own work,' says Claire Minton, a professional indexer in the novel *Cat's Cradle* by Kurt Vonnegut. 'It's a revealing thing [...] a shameless exhibition – to the trained eye. [...] Never index your own book.'*

* An index is a 'pointing finger' and the term has been used for both the manicule symbol ☞ and the familiar alphabetical list of a book's contents.

SEALING-WAX: in a drawer
134, on a table 133, up for
discussion 5
SENTENCES: dreadful
but brilliant 6, final 154,
prison 132
SEX: bad 10, circular 149,
criminal 92, oral 69,
the Second 45
SHARKS: long-nosed 131,
salt-sea 36
SHEEP: electric 40, 111,
sky-blue 95
SHIPS: avenging 119,
beguiling 5, hulking 123,
sustaining 84, tilting 4,
Viking 82
SHOES: in book titles 73,
in conversation 5, in transit
55; unworn 20
SHOPS: book 91, curiosity 98,
sheep's 147, wine 143,
work 44, 115, 123
SISTERS: Fossil 73, Little 137,
Stephen 126, Weird 36
SLEEP: after toil 152, at night
48, during the day 120,
in a bed 31, in a pint 7,
on a beach 72, on one's
own 140; the Big 137
SMELLS: of books 14,
of incense 140, of musty
lavatories 12, of new-cut hay
62, of the way the Taj Mahal
looks 137
SNAKES: divine 142, fenny 36
SNOW: in a chicken 148, in
Nebraska 101, in Wales 95;
White 16, 23
SOAP: branded 55, 58,
predatory 108
SOLDIERS: active 43, 149,
good 72, 78, 140, inactive 11,
tin 95
SOUP: pea 74, tortoise 25
SPARROWS: butchered 7,
maternal 140,
Shakespearean 33

SPIDERS: conspicuous 137,
feline 16, jumping 131,
monstrous 86
SPINACH: caged 14,
for wiping 59
STAMPS: municipal 7,
postage 24, 135, rubber 160
STARS: aimed for 160, little 18;
Gauge 44; Hour of the 51
STONES: brim 113, brown 73,
grave 17, 152, paving 6,
whet 41; charmed 76,
polished 133, talking 8, 30
STRAWBERRIES: unwelcome
62, welcome 112; juice 136
STRINGS: G- 73, shoe 139
TEETH: aching 26, biting 69,
clenched 145, cut 102,
lost 43, sharp 86, wolf's 36
TIME: lost 12, 46–7, 102,
regained 46, subsidized 58,
worshipped 142; to dance
10, 50, to die 50, to keep
silence 50, to kill 50, to love
50, to read 91, to write 68,
132; machines 20, 78; the
Dark Back of 71, the Music
of 46
TONGUES: canine 36,
demonic 145, hard 38,
missing 11, slithery 10,
unconstricted 126
TORTOISES: falling 150,
giant 25; and the Hare 32
TOWERS: drop 153, glass 41,
ivory 66, 151, Malory 65
UNDERCLOTHES: adult 58,
lace 96; G-strings 73
VOLCANOES: Popocatépetl
143, Vesuvius 139, 148
VULTURES: Nazi 60, pet 81
WALKING: alone 154, fast 139,
in Hell 48, in sandals 62,
with a lobster 81
WALRUSES: piratical 36, sly 5
WATER: margin 30, mark 54,
135, melon 112, pistols 136;
fire and 83, love of 48, milk

and 69, moon under 116,
written in 152; back 46,
boiling 123, tap 148, muddy
17, noisy 12, shower 19
WINE: canary 109, claret 123,
Médoc 62, quince 143
WITCHES: the three 36,
the worst 65
WIZARDS: Gandalf 33, 114,
Merlin 41
WOMEN: assembly 104,
blonde 137, free 105, little
60, old 14, 95, patronising
51, serious 73, Trojan 141,
young 139, 145; in slacks 62,
of pleasure 132, with dog's
eyes 121
WOODS: Holly 55, Milk 116,
'Wandring' 67; of suicides
122
WORDS: broken 145,
caged 14, deceptive 37,
four-letter 96, last 154, long
90, 104, stories with six 20,
thunder 15, unintelligible
105, useful 14
WORLDS: blazing 67,
circumnavigated 25, 101,
fictional 33, 100, 114,
floating 103, grown-up 138,
new 45, 92, perfect 103;
history of the 45, 132, war
of the 103; under 116
WORMS: blind 36, injured 48,
tape 102

THE AUTHOR AND PUBLISHERS GRATEFULLY ACKNOWLEDGE PERMISSION to reprint the following material: **6-7** Bulwer Lytton Fiction Contest winning entries, reprinted by permission of Scott Rice and bulwer-lytton.com; **10** *A Time to Dance* by Melvyn Bragg © 1990 Melvyn Bragg Ltd, reprinted by permission of Hodder & Stoughton (UK) and Peters Fraser & Dunlop (US), on behalf of Melvyn Bragg Ltd; *I Am Charlotte Simmons* by Tom Wolfe, Vintage; **12** *Proust* by Samuel Beckett © 1931 Samuel Beckett, reprinted by permission of Georges Borchardt, Inc., on behalf of the Estate of Samuel Beckett; **20** a short story by Margaret Atwood © 2006 O.W. Toad Ltd, which first appeared in *Wired Magazine*, reprinted by permission of Curtis Brown Group Ltd, London, on behalf of O.W. Toad Ltd; short stories by Arthur C. Clarke, Harry Harrison & Alan Moore from 'Very Short Stories', *Wired Magazine*, 1 Nov 2006; a short story by Colin Greenland, reprinted by permission of the author; a short story by Ursula K. Le Guin © 2006 Ursula K. Le Guin, *Wired Magazine*, reprinted by permission of Ginger Clark Literary, LLC; 'Widow's First Year' by Joyce Carol Oates, which first appeared in the *Ontario Review*; *Extraordinary Tales* by Jorge Luis Borges & Adolfo Bioy Casares, trans. Alberto Manguel, in *A History of Reading*, HarperCollins; **37** *The Meaning of Liff* and *The Deeper Meaning of Liff* by Douglas Adams & John Lloyd © 1983, 1990, 2013 Completely Unexpected Productions Ltd & John Lloyd, reprinted by permission of Macmillan and Curtis Brown Ltd, London, on behalf of Completely Unexpected Productions Ltd; **38-9** *The Sot-Weed Factor* by John Barth, Atlantic; **43** *The Twelve Caesars* by Suetonius, trans. Robert Graves, Penguin; **44** *I, Robot* by Isaac Asimov, HarperCollins; **55** 'The White Album' from *The White Album* by Joan Didion © 1979 Joan Didion, reprinted by permission of HarperCollins Publishers Ltd (UK) & Farrar, Straus and Giroux (US); **58** *Infinite Jest* by David Foster Wallace, Abacus; **62** *Roland Barthes* by Roland Barthes, Vintage; **68** *Henry Miller on Writing* by Henry Miller © 1944, 1957, 1964 Henry Miller © 1939, 1941, 1957 New Directions Publishing Corp; **69** *The Kama Sutra*, trans. A. N. D. Haksar, Penguin; **77** *Why Read the Classics?* by Italo Calvino, trans. Martin McLaughlin, Penguin; **79** 'Brief Notes on the Art and Manner of Arranging One's Books' in *Species of Spaces* by Georges Perec, trans. John Sturrock, Penguin; **86** *The Life of St Columba* by Adomnán of Iona, trans. Richard Sharpe, Penguin; *The Odyssey* by Homer, trans. E. V. Rieu & D. C. H. Rieu, Penguin; *Beowulf* by Seamus Heaney, Faber; *The Epic of Gilgamesh*, trans. Andrew George, Penguin; **91** *If on a winter's night a traveller* by Italo Calvino, trans. William Weaver, Vintage; **95** *A Child's Christmas in Wales* by Dylan Thomas, Orion; **96** *The Notebooks of Raymond Chandler* by Raymond Chandler © 1976 Helga Greene for the Estate of Raymond Chandler, reprinted by permission of HarperCollins Publishers and Rogers, Coleridge and White Ltd; **100** 'The Narrative Structure in Fleming' by Umberto Eco © 1966 Umberto Eco, in *Popular Culture: Past and Present*, ed. Bernard Waites et al, Routledge, reprinted by permission of Taylor and Francis Group, LLC, a division of Informa PLC; **112** *The Very Hungry Caterpillar* by Eric Carle, Puffin; **114** *The Lord of the Rings* by J. R. R. Tolkien, HarperCollins; **117** *The Total Library* by Jorge Luis Borges, ed. Eliot Weinberger, Penguin; **121** 'Death's Echo' in *Selected Poems* by W. H. Auden, Faber; *The Waste Land* in *Selected Poems* by T. S. Eliot, Faber; **128** *Timaeus* by Plato, trans. Desmond Lee, Penguin; **133** 'Notes Concerning the Objects that are on my Work-table' in *Species of Spaces* by Georges Perec, trans. John Sturrock, Penguin; **136** *Seven Types of Ambiguity* by William Empson, New Directions; **137** *Trouble is My Business, The Big Sleep, Farewell, My Lovely, The High Window, The Little Sister* and *The Long Good-bye* by Raymond Chandler, Vintage; **138** *Early Diaries, 1947–1963* by Susan Sontag, Penguin; **140** *The Pillow Book* by Sei Shōnagon, trans. Meredith McKinney, Penguin; **141** *Complete Nonsense* by Mervyn Peake, reprinted by kind permission of Carcanet Press, Manchester, UK; **144** 'Manifesto of Surrealism' by André Breton, trans. Richard Seaver & Helen R. Lane, in *100 Artists' Manifestos*, ed. Alex Danchev, Penguin; **145** *Molloy* by Samuel Beckett, trans. Samuel Beckett & Patrick Bowles © 1947 Les Editions Minuit, reprinted by permission of Faber and Faber Ltd and Georges Borchardt, Inc., on behalf of the Estate of Samuel Beckett; **145** *The Catcher in the Rye* by J. D. Salinger, Penguin; **154** *The Unnamable* by Samuel Beckett, trans. Samuel Beckett © 1953 Les Editions Minuit, reprinted by permission of Faber and Faber Ltd and Georges Borchardt, Inc., on behalf of the Estate of Samuel Beckett. Every effort has been made to contact all rights holders. The publishers will be pleased to amend in future editions any errors or omissions brought to their attention.

John Steinbeck signed off his letters with this 'Pigasus'
rubber stamp and the motto *Ad astra per alia porci*
('to the stars on the wings of a pig'). He saw himself
as Pigasus, 'a lumbering soul but trying to fly'.

And now for the most important list … I am extremely grateful to John Ash,
Katy Banyard, Thi Dinh, Olivia Eliot, Simon Eliot, Sandra Fuller, Sam Fulton,
Fergus Hardy, Georgina Hardy, Jessica Harrison, Lindsay Johns, Taryn Jones,
Rebecca Lee, Matt Lloyd-Rose, Stefan McGrath, Ingrid Matts, Jon Parker, Ed Posnett,
Kit Shepherd, Kate Smith, Patrick Walsh, Louise Willder, Andy Wimbush and
Dahmicca Wright. Thank you all. Special thanks to Richard Atkinson, my editor,
and Matthew Young, the designer and illustrator: you have been brilliant collab-
orators, pouring wit, enthusiasm and time into every page. I am enormously
grateful to you both. And finally, many thanks to Georgie and Toby, to whom
this book is jointly dedicated, for their love and support as always.

PARTICULAR BOOKS
UK | USA | Canada | Ireland | Australia
India | New Zealand | South Africa

 Penguin
Random House
UK

Penguin Books is part of the Penguin Random
House group of companies
whose addresses can be found at global.
penguinrandomhouse.com

First published in Great Britain
by Particular Books 2022
001
Text copyright © Henry Eliot, 2022
The moral right of the author has been asserted

Typeset by Matthew Young in 9.5/13pt Garalda
Printed and bound in Great Britain by Clays Ltd,
Elcograf S.p.A.

The authorized representative in the EEA is
Penguin Random House Ireland, Morrison
Chambers, 32 Nassau Street, Dublin DO2 YH68

A CIP catalogue record for this book is available
from the British Library
ISBN: 978-0-241-56272-7

www.greenpenguin.co.uk